Grandparents
WISCONSIN STYLE

by Mike Link and Kate Crowley

Adventure Publications, Inc.
Cambridge, Minnesota

Dedication:

To Matthew, Aren, Ryan and Annalise, who have taught us the magic of grandparenting.

You're responsible for your own safety and well-being. Make good choices out there.

Photo credits:

Cover photos: Camp 5 Museum Foundation: train (back cover, middle inset) National Fresh Water Fishing Hall of Fame: fish museum close-up (back cover, middle-right inset) Wisconsin Cranberry Discovery Center: front cover (middle inset) All other cover photos courtesy of Mike Link and Kate Crowley

All photos are copyright Mike Link and Kate Crowley unless otherwise noted. Camp 5 Museum Foundation: 102 America's Black Holocaust Museum: 30 Lake Superior Big Top Chautauqua: 100 Joseph Mischka: 66 Bristol Renaissance Faire: 46 National Fresh Water Fishing Hall of Fame: 88 Prairie du Chien Tourism Council: 64 Shutterstock: 18, 28, 36, 50, 86, 104, 106, 126, 128, 148, 150, 152, 154, 156 Wisconsin Rapids Area Convention & Visitors Bureau: 80

Cover and book design by Jonathan Norberg
Illustrations by Brenna Slabaugh

10 9 8 7 6 5 4 3 2 1

Contents

Introduction

Grandparents Wisconsin Style is designed for today's grandparent who wants to spend more time discovering the world with his or her grandchildren. This book is about opportunities for adult and child to have fun, laugh and share. Of course, Wisconsin is ripe with more possibilities than we can ever cover, but this is a place to get you started. We decided to write this book because of our grandchildren—three boys and a girl. They provide us with a lot of fun, but we also have a responsibility to them. We must use our time together to help them learn and grow as individuals.

In successfully doing so, we had to stop and think about the knowledge we've gained through our experiences, how we learned those valuable life lessons and how we could pass our wisdom to our grandchildren. With the changing times, we found that several necessary experiences have become endangered. Some of them include solitude, silence, open space, dark night skies, free time, reading books, family meals and home-cooked food.

Several differences within our society have contributed to our grandchildren's diminished opportunities. Consider the following:

1. In 1900, farmers accounted for forty percent of our census. By 1990, the total fell below two percent. Farms are no longer a part of most children's experiences.

2. Open space was once a playground. Now it is slated for development. Children are left with only fenced yards and indoor locations.

3. The "out in the country" experience is disappearing. Urban sprawl has left us with an hour drive from the inner city to any country areas.

4. Tree climbing is a thing of the past. The trees are all but gone, and lawsuits limit access to just about everything. There is nothing left to take the modern Jacks and Jills up the beanstalk to their dreams.

5. The chance to be bored—which is an opportunity to be creative—isn't in the schedule. Children are signed up for every organized activity and training available, eliminating family time and free time.

6. Sports used to be played for fun. Now we must choose a sport, send our kids to summer camps and act like winning is all that matters.

7. Canning, pickling and baking—all of those wonderful activities that filled the root-cellars and pantries of the past—have vanished.

Think about our earlier years, about all of the things that were so important to our lives and developments. These and many more are gone (or nearly so), and we can only reminisce about their absences: soda fountains, radio dramas, family TV, typewriters, telephone party lines, the ragman driving his horse cart, ice cream trucks and record players.

Today's world has seen some bad and dangerous trends. Pollution has become an industry. Fast food (and obesity) is the norm. Meth and other deadly drugs flood our cities, our neighborhoods and our schools. And that's just the tip of the iceberg.

There are no simple solutions, yet the need for change is quite apparent. Fortunately, our grandchildren have us. The role of the grandparent is very different than it was when we were young kids, and we must adapt too. Here are a few reasons why:

1. Grandparents are living longer than ever before and can guide their grandchildren longer.

2. Parents work long days, filled with busy hours.

3. Grandparents can provide children with quiet times, new experiences, fewer electronics and more play.

4. Grandparents can help introduce children to healthier food; we have the time to prepare it and present it.

5. Children need to hear perspectives from someone other than peers and parents. They need our guidance and insight.

It comes down to a need to establish the extended family again, the new nuclear family of the twenty-first century. As grandparents, we must take it upon ourselves to lead the charge.

That's not to say we should take on the role of mother and father. Instead our place is to supplement a child's parents, to help them wherever our help is wanted and needed. Let's use the time we have with our grandchildren to instill them with important values, to teach them about the world around them and to help shape them into better people.

A Word from Mike Link

"Where are you, Dad?"

"We got a late start and have about an hour till we get to you, why?"

"Well you better hurry. Your grandson heard Gampa was coming and now we're sitting out on the curb waiting for you to arrive."

An hour later we found our greeting party on the curb, on the blanket. Who could ask for a better welcome than that? That's the love our grandchildren have for us if we are willing to involve ourselves in their lives, the reason we want to create special memories with our grandchildren. Our greatest gift to them is our love and attention. They are the greatest gift we could receive.

What ancestors gave us:

The role of the grandparent is significant and played an important part in the lives of Kate, me and our children. I spent all of my "non-school" time living with my grandparents in Rice Lake, while my father worked evenings and week-ends to try to get us out of poverty. It was not a desertion of responsibility but rather a sharing. I was born in Rice Lake. My father and mother moved to Minnesota for work, but in spirit they never really left Wisconsin.

My dad worked second shift, from 3 p.m. to midnight, and that meant we had little time together, so my grandfather taught me to play catch, to drive, to work. He was my partner. My grandmother picked berries with me, taught me the pleasure of fresh-baked pies and cookies. Both of them were there to guide me, to share with me, and to set an example.

I was also lucky to know my great grandparents and to see my heritage through this multi-level set of grandparents. It was a wonderful way to connect time and generations. In some ways it was a tradition begun before I came along. My great-great-grandmother, Ogima Benisi Kwe (Chief Bird Woman) was from the La Court O'Reilles reservation; she married my great-great-grandfather John Quaderer, fresh from Liechtenstein. He had entered the country through New Orleans, come up the Mississippi, and ended up in the Chippewa River Valley.

Their daughter, Anna Kahl, my great-grandmother, was a wonderful woman who raised not only her thirteen children on their Prairie Farm farm, but also five of my uncles who moved back to the reservation as they reached adulthood. She carried forward the tradition that a grandparent should be the role model and the teacher, while the parents provide safety, home, food and other provisions. She is part of who I am, part of my connection with the world.

My grandmother Prock's kolaches were the connection to our Czech heritage. Sauerkraut, roast pork and mashed potatoes were an extension of our German heritage. The extension of my *Anishanabe* heritage created the succession of grandparent/grandchild roles and bonds that continue today. I believe that the extended role of the traditional grandparent is one that fits today's needs.

What we can give grandchildren:

In an age when "Soccer Mom" and "Soccer Dad" are normal terms to describe parenting, we are in a confusion of roles and relationships. Often parents are scheduling rather than parenting, channeling rather than nurturing. Our society has caused some parents to allow others to "coach" their children into maturity. This may not be the parent's choice, but in the driven world we have created, the demands to make a living are great.

Do not despair; there is a solution that is ancient. In a *Washington Post* editorial Abigail Trafford describes the plight of today's families; she refers to the next two decades as the transition from baby boomers to grand baby boomers.

Today grandparents live longer, have the potential for better health and more opportunities than ever before to share their stories, read books, look at old photo albums, talk about the good old days and enjoy their grandchildren. But what to do? Talking, reading and photo albums are all great, but the stories are wonderful because you lived them, the photos have meaning because you experienced something that the photo reminds you of.

If you want to build memories rather than dwelling on them, get out, get going, take those grandchildren and experience the world again for the first time through their smiles, their curiosity, their wonder and their energy.

In a 1996 book, *Contemporary Grandparenting*, Arthur Kornhaber, M.D., shows the evolution of individuals from their own childhood to grandparenting:

- from receiving as a child to giving as an elder
- from being nurtured as a child to nurturing the young
- from learning to teaching
- from listening to stories to telling them
- from being directed to directing
- from simply reacting to one's environment to becoming able to influence the world
- from identifying with others to becoming an object of identification

We are the elders; we are the starting point for more generations. How exciting and how challenging. But don't dwell on responsibility. Just be yourself. Be honest, be fun, be open. Grandchildren are gifts from the future and through them we can see the decades ahead—they connect us to their world and we in turn owe them a connection to ours.

A Word from Kate Crowley

If you're lucky, you grew up knowing your grandparents. If you're even luckier those grandparents lived nearby and enriched your life by their interest and enthusiastic involvement. Unfortunately, the Industrial Revolution, while it has brought us lives of relative ease and abundance, has also brought about the gradual decline and demise of the close-knit, extended family.

Much of the knowledge that our elders, the grandparents, carried was tied to life on the land. We can recall the easy, simple times spent with these adults who indulged us and shared their memories of a time that today seems as remote and as removed as the Middle Ages. Yet, since we carry the memories and experiences with us, we have the opportunity to share them with a new generation, being born into a century with untold opportunities and far too many dangers.

As we age, we reflect on our childhoods. Even though the mists of time tend to spray a cloud of gold over those days, we know there were experiences that gave us great pleasure and cemented the bonds with the elders who shared themselves with us.

When I was born, I had two living grandmothers. One lived in California, and I have very fuzzy memories of her. She only visited us a handful of times, and I don't recall her as particularly warm or even interested in interacting with my siblings or me.

My other grandmother lived just a block away from us, and I had more than twenty years of close acquaintance with her. I even lived with her for four years during and after high school. She didn't have the time or personality to get down on the floor and play with us, but her house was always open to us and we wore a path through our neighbor's backyards to get there. She had a few old toys and books for us to play with and a big, old piano that we made noise on, but mostly we simply came over to visit. If we were lucky, she'd make us root beer floats.

This is what I believe about our most firmly held memories of time with our grandparents: They are tied to our senses, all of which were much keener for us as children. Smell, sight, sound, touch and taste—these are the things that will stay with a child as they grow to adulthood, recalling times shared with grandparents.

One of the most mouth-watering, sensual memories I have with my grandmother is from a summer day, when we went out into the country to pick tomatoes. It was a hot day and even though we got there early, the sun was beating down on us as we moved through the pungent rows of tomato plants. What I remember most about the day is that she packed cheese sandwiches— most likely Velveeta—and I have never eaten anything more delicious than a rich, sweet tomato right off the vine, still holding the sun's heat, juice running down my chin, followed by a bite of soft cheese on white bread. The smells and tastes flowed together, and I can see us there now, joined forever by the simple act of harvesting food.

I have waited a very long time to become a grandmother and not just because our daughters chose to wait until their thirties to have children. I can't explain why, but even when my two children were preteens, I was contemplating grandparenthood. I packed away all of their Fisher Price toys in the original boxes to share with the next generation, and I saved as many of their books as possible. I so greatly enjoyed raising those two children that I knew I wanted to have similar experiences again—but without the many worries and day-to-day concerns that accompany parenthood. I understood even then that, as a grandparent, I would be able to have fun, play, act silly and share what I've learned in life but still have the luxury of going home at the end of the day to a quiet, clean house.

Now we have three grandsons and a granddaughter—all of whom arrived in the span of four years—and we are looking forward to years of adventures together. This is why we've written *Grandparents Wisconsin Style*: to help other grandparents find those unique and unforgettable places that will combine fun and facts, history and humor, excitement and enduring memories for you and for the special grandchildren in your life.

How to Use This Book

The suggestions in this book are just that: suggestions. Some experiences are unmatchable anywhere else in the state. Others can be replicated. If you are not near the museum, park or site that we highlight, find a similar place near you. Read our suggestions, and be sure to pay special attention to each "Bonding and bridging." This is how we believe you can tie your visit to an important life lesson. Take advantage of our advice or come up with your own, but use each opportunity to its fullest!

We do not advocate that you become the "wallet" or the "chauffeur." What we want you to consider is an active participation in friendship and sharing that is enriched by love. We want you to receive the respect of an elder, to exhibit the wisdom of your age and experience, and to enjoy the wonderful love that can flow between generations.

One of the themes of this book is that things change. This is true for every-thing, including our state's attractions. They sometimes close, renovate or move. When in doubt, *CALL BEFORE YOU LEAVE*.

Lake Michigan Beaches

The longest of the Great Lakes shorelines is Lake Michigan, a north-south shoreline that technically starts at the Michigan border, goes around the Door County Peninsula, and then sweeps down past Sheboygan, Kohler-Andrae State Park, Milwaukee, Kenosha and on to Chicago. The lake is a long tube that resembles a lady's slipper flower in shape. It is 307 miles long and 118 miles wide. There is a lot to know and a lot to explore on a lake of this size. It is the third largest of the U.S. Great Lakes and the sixth largest in the world.

With this much area, there are multiple options for exploration, but for children, nothing is more inviting than long sandy beaches, and fortunately many of these have been preserved through state and local parks. Start with Newport State Park in Door County for a quiet and remote beach. Move to Whitefish Dunes for massive, pristine dune ecology, plus a sweep of sand ripe for building sand castles, running along the edge of incoming waves, having picnics, sunbathing and playing in the water. As in all the state parks and forests, there are campsites here if you are inclined to spend more than the day.

Down the shore at the end of the peninsula is Point Beach State Forest with six miles of beach to investigate. In Sheboygan, a city park encompasses a magnificent flat beach with lots of room to roam and a nice bike and hiking trail. Kohler-Andrae State Park has a wonderful interpretive center, two miles of sandy beach and a playground. Harrington Beach State Park offers yet another mile of excellent beach.

Along the southern part of Lake Michigan, Milwaukee has a great shoreline with biking and hiking trails and lots of places to explore, like the Betty Brinn Children's Museum, Milwaukee Art Museum, and Discovery World. And even farther south, Kenosha has a small island connected to the mainland by bridge, a sandy beach, a lighthouse, a picnic area and a channel to bring in recreational boats.

It hardly needs saying, but grandchildren love to play in the sand and surf. It's universal. A few cheap shovels and buckets, sunscreen and towels, a little drinking water in a cooler and a few snacks promise a great beach day.

Bonding and bridging:

What is it about waves, water and sand that are so relaxing and inviting? Ask your grandchildren. Help them understand how wonderful it is that others have preserved these areas. What can they do that will help keep the beaches beautiful and clean? Maybe you can help them pick up some litter and talk about how we all share responsibilities for public areas. One of the great things about the U.S. is that we were wise enough to put some places in the hands of the "commons"—that is, everybody. What would we do if the beaches were only owned by a few individuals?

A word to the wise:

The sun feels so good, how could it possibly be bad? That's the thinking of a lot of adults, especially in the northern hemisphere where we are so hungry for sunlight after winter. But grandparents know what happens over a lifetime of tans and burns. Many parents today are aware of the dangers that sunburn poses to our grandchildren, so most kids are used to the routine of putting on sunscreen when going outdoors. Still, it doesn't hurt for us to reinforce the practice.

Age of grandchild: All

Best season: Summer

Contact:

Kohler-Andrae State Park, 1020 Beach Park Lane,
Sheboygan, WI 53081 • (920) 451-4080 • www.dnr.state.wi.us

Newport State Park, 475 County Highway NP,
Ellison Bay, WI 54210 • (920) 854-2500 • www.dnr.state.wi.us

Point Beach State Forest, 9400 County Highway O,
Two Rivers, WI 54241 • (920) 794-7480 • www.dnr.state.wi.us

Whitefish Dunes State Park, 3275 Clark Lake Road,
Sturgeon Bay, WI 54235 • (920) 823-2400 • www.dnr.state.wi.us

Also check out:

Big Bay State Park on Madeline Island, Bayfield: www.dnr.state.wi.us

Grandparents, like heroes, are as necessary to a child's growth as vitamins. JOYCE ALLSTON

Door County Bicycle Trails

Two of the best bike trails in Wisconsin give you and your grandchildren a pleasant and healthy way to see the contrasts of the famous Door County Peninsula. This is Wisconsin's favorite vacation paradise, but people often forget that it is the quiet beauty, the bays and points, that provide inspiration for contemplation, and the beauty of the green landscape within the embrace of Green Bay and Lake Michigan that makes it special. Get your grandchildren away from the roads, the crowds and the cash registers and put them on bikes. Let them get healthy and inspired.

Peninsula State Park bike trails are just one of many special features of this premier park. The trails are on designated roads and on "bike only" gravel trails. There are some hills, so that needs to be considered, but overall it is a pleasure for most family members to pedal here. The bike seems the perfect vehicle for exploring, stopping and relaxing. The Sunset Trail accommodates bicycles, wheelchairs and hikers so you know it is suitable for the family and is a nice trail to combine with the Shore Road. Only 5.1 miles long, the trail manages to include marshes, upland hardwoods and conifer stands.

Bikes and boats seem to have little in common, but the Ahnapee State Trail (beginning near Potawatomi State Park) connects the shipping lanes and the Great Lakes freighters in Sturgeon Bay to the fishing boats in Algoma as the

trail follows the Ahnapee River. The trail is thirty-one miles long, with a small section paralleling the river. Trailriders will see the Ahnapee Wildlife Refuge and the Forestville Millpond. In addition, there are rock exposures of the Niagara Escarpment and the rural beauty of orchards and dairy farms. The lack of major grades makes it a very nice place for families to pedal.

The two trails can be covered in two days and give the grandchildren a real sense of the landscape that attracts people here year after year. It also gives grandparents a combination of things to explore, both manmade and natural. Combine the natural areas with the communities. Fish Creek offers the unique architecture and New England style community that people expect on the Door. At the end of the Ahnapee State Trail, Algoma is a wonderful contrast to Sturgeon Bay. End here with a stroll on the boardwalk or an exploration of Crescent Beach.

Bonding and bridging:

What makes a place special? Why do people like to come to Door County? It is a good idea for grandparents to talk about likes and dislikes. Why is one toy better than another? Why do we like one piece of art more than another? You can explore what your grandchildren like and help them to form opinions about what they might choose in the future.

It is easy to be caught in the excitement of fast and loud things, but it takes time to understand how quiet, calm places make us feel better and add to our joy of life. Our lives are richer when we have a variety of experiences and pleasures.

A word to the wise:

Children are no better judge of their condition than are adults, and we all tend to overestimate how much we can do. So before you go on a trip and jump on your bikes, think about what you could do to get ready. Maybe a few short rides near home first would be good. We all need exercise, but when we overdo it, that sets us back further than any gain a long ride might give us.

Age of grandchild: 10 and up

Best season: Late spring through early fall

Contact:

Ahnapee State Trail, Kewaunee County Promotion and Recreation Department, E4280 County F, Kewaunee, WI 54216
(920) 388-0444 • www.ahnapeetrail.org

Peninsula State Park, 9462 Shore Road, Fish Creek, WI 54212
(920) 868-3258 • www.dnr.state.wi.us

Also check out:

400 State Trail, Reedsburg: www.400statetrail.org

Elroy-Sparta State Trail, Kendall: www.elroy-sparta-trail.com

La Crosse River State Trail, Sparta: www.lacrosseriverstatetrail.org

Find a Wisconsin State Trail:
www.dnr.state.wi.us/org/land/parks/specific/findatrail.html

Just when I thought I was too old to fall in love again, I became a Grandparent. Unknown

Door County
Maritime Museum

This extraordinary museum began its life on Gills Rock at the end of the Door County Peninsula in 1969 because a group of professional fishermen saw the need to capture the heritage of this seafaring county. Many people think of Wisconsin as a landlocked state in the middle of the continent, but a quick look at a map of North America shows the extensive shorelines on both Lake Superior and Lake Michigan. Here you can help your grandchildren discover this exciting part of Wisconsin's history.

Door County Peninsula is the famous thumb of Wisconsin, because it juts out into the waters of Lake Michigan. It divides an otherwise linear lake into Green Bay and the main lake. With a ship canal extending from the waters of Sturgeon Bay all the way across the peninsula, northern Door County has become an island, tied to the cold and demanding waters that surround it. It was so dramatic that the name Door is a short version of the original—Death's Door—the name that described its hazards for early shipping.

Your grandchildren can trace the history of shipping from the dugout boat to world-famous yachts and relate to the models that show us what the ships look like. Grandchildren will enjoy these scale models that bring the story to their level of understanding.

Shipbuilding, recreational boating, the Coast Guard and the lighthouses of this region are all featured in a history that is presented well and filled with surprises. Watch the videos with the kids, talk about what they see and hear, and explore the boats both inside and outside the building.

Let your imagination flow as you move among old-fashioned cruise boats, among desks and chairs in the office of the shipping company, and into a ship's pilothouse. My favorite is the engine room, with the complex machinery from large ships contrasting with a row of small outboard engines.

End outside where the children see the boats in the water, the size, color and variations in shapes. What would it be like to work, to travel, or to immigrate to the U.S. on a boat? Whether it was Eric the Red, Chinese explorers or Christopher Columbus who was the non-Indian discoverer of North America, you know that it was a boat that brought the world together from its Flat Earth beginnings.

Bonding and bridging:

Boats were the equivalent of spaceships and airplanes for most of human history. They were the vessels that extended civilization and allowed the expansion of culture, wealth and nations. Sit by the water and talk about what it must have been like for explorers to set out when the philosophers of the day thought the Earth was flat and they might go off the edge. How frightening must it have been for people to pack up all their belongings in a trunk and set sail for another continent to create a living and a future? How did the canoe support the lifestyle of the Native Americans and what happened when they shared this marvelous craft with the French, English and Canadians? You might think about either building a model boat or taking a good toy boat to a pond to help your grandchild connect with the beauty and utility of boats.

A word to the wise:

Wisconsin has nearly a thousand miles of Great Lakes shoreline. Every island or peninsula extends the shoreline, and so far no one has been able to map the landscape with all its little coves and nooks. Maps have been tools for every traveler from the drawings on caves through our satellite-generated photo maps. When you have an experience like this, where transportation is so key to the understanding, it is a good opportunity to get out a map and start to find locations, distance and perspective. Like the models in the museum, the map is an attempt to make the scale something we can grasp.

Age of grandchild: 5 and up

Best season: All

Contact: Door County Maritime Museum, 120 North Madison Avenue, Sturgeon Bay, WI 54235 • (920) 743-5958 • www.dcmm.org

Also check out:

Cana Island Lighthouse, Cana Island: www.dcmm.org/canaisland.html

Eagle Bluff Lighthouse, Fish Creek: www.eagleblufflighthouse.org

Museum at Gills Rock, Gills Rock: www.dcmm.org/gillsrock.html

Wisconsin Maritime Museum, Manitowoc: www.wisconsinmaritime.org

Perfect love sometimes does not come until grandchildren are born. WELSH PROVERB

Cherry Picking
in Door County

What is more American than apple pie? Maybe it is the cherry pie. After all one of America's great myths has George Washington chopping down a cherry tree. Now cherries are the bloom that dominates Washington, D.C., in the spring, and the ripe red cherries festoon the shrubs of Door County all summer. Of course the capital's cherries were actually a gift from Japan in 1912.

You can explore the orchards of Door County and taste both cherries and apples. When you do, you are participating in a tradition that goes back to the 1800s, when settlers discovered that the warm days and the cool nights on this Lake Michigan peninsula were perfect for fruit trees. Today there are more than 2,000 acres of cherry orchards and 1,000 acres of apples making it seem like a celebration, whether it is the flower or the fruit on the branches.

You can buy apples and cherries from fruit stands along the roads, but as we continue to stress, hands-on is the best. There will be cherries that all ages of grandchildren can pick and the labor of your work might be rewarded by a wonderful burst of cherry in your mouth. Your grandchildren will be engaged by seeing their buckets fill up, and you will be introducing them to a wonderfully healthy fruit. The average American eats about one pound of cherries per year and Wisconsin produces four percent nationally.

It is a festive time for you and your grandchildren. At one orchard there is a cherry spitting pit where you can attempt to set a world or personal record. Another way to enhance the experience is to time your picking with Jacksonport's Cherry Fest on the first Saturday in August. This event will provide you with lots of treats like fresh-baked cherry kolaches, cherry chip cookies, cherry pie and ice cream. The festival also has wagon rides and folk music, plus a penny hunt for children on the beach. Since cherry picking is slang for collecting erroneous coins, it fits the season and the festival.

The fresh air, the color and the setting are all aspects of the gathering that will stay with your grandchildren. This is what they will remember and share with their children. We would call it an agri-cultural event.

Bonding and bridging:

There are native cherries you can collect with your grandchildren to make jams and jellies. Choke-cherry, pin cherry and sand cherry shrubs all produce a wonderful fruit, but do not let your grandchildren think they will experience the sweet sensation of the domestic cherry—something that was brought to America by the early settlers in the 1600s.

Our food comes from all over the world and is combined in our gardens to give us great variety. Gathering wild berries is a wonderful way to bond with your grandchildren. It is one of the greatest sharing events you can do, especially if you work together to produce baked goods, ice cream sundaes, fruit and cream and other great combinations. As grandchildren get older they will never find anything that tastes as good as these treats—we grandparents know from experience.

A word to the wise:

The cherry is not only delicious, but it is also filled with the antioxidants that we grandparents are seeking. The Montmorency tart cherries have high oxygen radical absorption capacity (ORAC) and that makes them a powerful elixir for us as we grow older—good for our grandchildren and good for us, too!

Age of grandchild: 5 and up

Best season: Mid-July through late August

Contact:

Cherry Lane Orchards, 7525 Cherry Lane, Sturgeon Bay, WI 54235 (920) 856-6864 • www.cherrylaneorchards.com

Hyline Orchards, 8240 State Highway 42, Fish Creek, WI 54212 (920) 868-3067 • www.hylineorchards.com

Le Fevre Orchards, 2600 Idlewild Road, Sturgeon Bay, WI 54235 (920) 737-2614

Also check out:

Jacksonport Cherry Fest, Jacksonport: www.doorbell.net/jhs/events.htm

Wisconsin Cherry Growers: www.wisconsincherries.org

Lambeau Field and
the Packers Hall of Fame

Maybe it is because I was born in Wisconsin and all my family lived in Wisconsin that I entered high school with a feeling that the Green Bay Packers were my local team. As time goes on my loyalties have been shifted by time, place and circumstance, but a visit to Lambeau Field is the antidote for any doubt about where the Packers belong in America's consciousness.

The NFL began in 1923, a League that pulled together teams from struggling associations and organizations. Only two teams from that group are still in the NFL—the Packers and the Bears! If you and your grandchildren are football fans, even a little, this is the place to come.

Talk about pride—professional football players in the smallest town in the NFL! Real people meet real players. We do not specifically recommend professional sports venues in most states because those are commercial ventures which represent the world of sport and not the community, but this is different. In smalltown Green Bay, it is like David versus Goliath. We cannot imagine a town of this size ever being awarded a pro sports franchise in the future.

It does not have to be a game day to get a special feeling, with giant statues of famous coaches Curly Lambeau and Vince Lombardi looking down at you as you enter. It is like going to Mount Olympus in another era, only here the legends are not named Mars, Mercury, Jupiter and Zeus, but everywhere you look are the names of football legends: Nitschke, Hornung, Hudson, Favre and White.

No football game? So what. There will be smaller crowds and more time to explore and have fun. There is a gift store that feels like a museum and a Hall of Fame that is a museum. The Green Bay Packers Hall of Fame is like the doorway to the NFL Hall of Fame since the league history is only as old as the team history.

While grandparents might enjoy reading the displays, exploring the stories and watching the videos, the grandchildren will have fun in the locker room—a place set aside for football dreams and imagination.

Bonding and bridging:

People like to say that we can learn about life through sports and that is true if someone is your guide. Sports stars are amazing athletes, but that does not make them good people. In today's world we too often give people respect for the wrong things—strength, money, power. But how do grandchildren understand this? It is up to you to give them perspective.

Do the athletes help them cross the street? Do they make the city safe, put out fires, teach important things? No. Athletes play a role in our society. They entertain. It is a good role, but not essential. The real heroes may not be on the gridiron, or the diamond, or the oval, or any of the other geometric symbols that abound in sports. The heroes are the people who make life better. So we can celebrate the athletes, enjoy their victories and hopefully avoid letting their defeats depress us. Perspective is hard to come by, but essential to a good life. We honor those who contribute to others' lives.

A word to the wise:

Ask your grandchildren to tell you what a hero is. The halls of fame are filled with athletic prowess, but see if you can find the stories about the athletes who rose above the sport and helped the community. Find the qualities in sports that are important to everyone, in every line of work—intelligence, dedication, practice, knowledge, teamwork. Then emphasize those qualities as you enjoy thinking about the Packer champions and championships.

Age of grandchild: 10 and up

Best season: All

Contact: Green Bay Packers Hall of Fame, 1265 Lombardi Avenue, Green Bay, WI 54304 • (920) 569-7512 • www.packers.com/hall_of_fame

Also check out:

International Clown Hall of Fame, West Allis: www.theclownmuseum.org

National Fresh Water Fishing Hall of Fame & Museum, Hayward: www.freshwater-fishing.org

Wisconsin Conservation Hall of Fame, Stevens Point: www.wchf.org

EAA AirVenture Oshkosh

To fly like the birds has been a dream of humans since we learned that our bodies were tightly held to the Earth. For centuries people imagined human flight and Leonardo da Vinci came up with some very good designs, but it wasn't until our own grandparents were young that the dream became reality.

How old were you when you went on your first airplane ride? Many of today's grandkids have already logged thousands of miles before their first birthdays.

Certainly airplanes are not something they are surprised to see, yet we all, regardless of age, still thrill to see just what these flying machines can do. That's really the main reason to go to the EAA AirVenture—"the world's greatest aviation celebration." Begun in 1953, the event has grown through the decades so that today over 700,000 people attend and 10,000 airplanes are part of the event. This weeklong event is like a combination State Fair and outdoor museum. You can choose to visit for just one day or for the whole week; just realize that if you plan to stay for more than one day, you will need to make hotel reservations months in advance.

Airplanes of all shapes, sizes and vintages are spread across the grounds, but the real highlight of this event is the afternoon air show. Bring a blanket or folding chairs and find a spot on the grass next to the airstrip. There are single-engine planes that fly solo, doing "loop de loops," squadrons of biplanes that do synchronized dives and barrel rolls, daredevil wing walkers and huge military transports that stun us with their size and maneuverability. Every day there is a different lineup of performers.

If your grandchildren get antsy, you can get up, gather your gear and wander off to look at the hundreds of planes parked throughout the expansive grounds, and talk to the people who fly them. There is also a "Theater in the Woods" where every evening there is a special program—anything from films related to flight, to musicians or aviation legends.

The kids will really enjoy a visit to KidVenture. This large tent is set up near the museum and here they can get involved in hands-on activities—from building a rocket to learning to fly a control-line model airplane to sitting in a simulator and pretending they're the pilot.

Bonding and bridging:

Dreams—both those we have at night and during our waking hours—can have an impact on our lives. Have you ever had a sleep dream where you felt like you were actually flying? Has your grandchild? We can talk about what that might mean.

What about our daydreams? Is flying an airplane something either one of you has dreamed about doing? For your grandchild, this could become a reality, but as with any such dream, there has to be an accompanying effort—whether study, saving money or working with others who are already living the dream. Share with your grandchild a dream you had as a child. Let them know that dreams do come true, for those who hold onto them and help bring them to life.

A word to the wise:

While the AirVenture is the reason most people come to Oshkosh each year, there is a permanent museum on the site with one of the most extensive aviation collections in the world. It is open all year, so you don't have to wait for the summer event to visit. There are more than 250 historic airplanes and over 20,000 historic aviation objects. The section that you won't want to miss, though, is the Family Flightfest (check website for dates) where there are interactive activities for kids of all ages. We waited in line for several minutes in order to try out the hang-glider simulator. It might actually be hard to pull your grandchildren away from this part of the museum.

Age of grandchild: 9 and up

Best season: Late July

Contact: EAA Aviation Center, 3000 Poberezny Road, Oshkosh, WI 54902 • (920) 426-4800 • www.airventure.org

Also check out:

Astrowings of Wisconsin, Grafton: www.astrowings.com

Mitchell Gallery of Flight, Milwaukee: www.mitchellgallery.org

Richard I. Bong World War II Heritage Center, Superior: www.bongheritagecenter.org

John Michael Kohler Arts Center

The Kohler Arts Center begins as soon as you enter the property. From the large chair statue that serves as the museum sign, you can walk around the block and shift from landscape to ruins, with art tucked in and around every corner. The playful attitude of the landscape and facility make it a perfect place to bring your grandchildren.

Not many places count their bathrooms as art, but this center does! Of course the Kohlers are the bathroom fixture family and the economic bedrock of Sheboygan, so it should be no surprise that the walls, the fixtures and even the ceiling are incorporated into the expressive artwork of the museum. We would have to rate these the number one bathrooms in the country and defy anyone to come up with better.

But there's more to this place than bathrooms. As you enter you will have the gift store to your right and the highlight of the museum for grandparents and for grandchildren on the left—the ARTery.

Docents are available to help your family explore the options in the ARTery: materials, tables, and a wonderfully inspiring room where your grandchildren

can let their creativity flow. Use clay, paints and crayons. This is one of the most kid-friendly art rooms we have seen.

Visit the displays and let the children see the variety of forms exhibited in this well-planned building. Often there is an artist in residence, so the children can connect the art work on the walls with the real person.

The exhibits change regularly so returning is a must, but the strength of the museum is in the variety of art forms exhibited, combined with the performing arts that they schedule for both formal and informal presentations. In addition, they offer many classes that help aspiring artists, and produce events with the local community that involve people of all ages.

A good way to conclude is to go to the ARTcafe, where you can enjoy a very nice lunch or get a seat for the early evening meal and music combination that explores the world through international performers and cuisine.

Bonding and bridging:

Creativity is a release of our inner self. In many ways the world stifles this creativity and that is a shame. Artists work hard for little money to maintain their expression, and your grandchildren may not know how precious this freedom is. So help them play with their ideas. Be supportive in the ARTery. Encourage, suggest and applaud. Grab a piece of paper and create with them. Don't direct them; let your creativity out, while they enjoy theirs.

You might find a little art corner in your home where grandchildren can put their finest creations. Let them understand that the art corner will change. Talk about how the exhibits do not have all the works of any one artist or style. They represent something special just as their own art represents who they are and what they think. Let them choose what to display and give them a place for artistic expression.

A word to the wise:

Have fun with the exhibits. Most of us are not trained critics and we need not pretend to be. Look at the art with your grandchildren and have fun. Be inspired by some, shocked by others, and laugh when you think something is funny. There is no rule that says all art is serious. Some works are just beyond us, but that is okay. In the act of looking at the art and observing the details we have fun. If it isn't fun, your grandchildren will not return, nor will you.

Age of grandchild: 5 and up

Best season: All

Contact: John Michael Kohler Arts Center, 608 New York Avenue, Sheboygan, WI 53081 • (920) 458-6144 • www.jmkac.org

Also check out:

Chazen Museum of Art, Madison: www.chazen.wisc.edu

Leigh Yawkey Woodson Art Museum, Wausau: www.lywam.org

Milwaukee Art Museum, Milwaukee: www.mam.org

Museum of Wisconsin Art, West Bend: www.wbartmuseum.com

I like to do nice things for my grandchildren—like buy them those toys I've always wanted to play with. GENE PERRET

Horicon Marsh

You hear them before you see them, which is to be expected when there are as many as 200,000 Canada geese at a time in the marshy waters. Every autumn, one million geese stream down from their tundra nesting grounds and land in this 32,000-acre cattail marsh. For many adults, seeing Canada geese may not be special, since the birds have come back very successfully from their near disappearance fifty years ago. But for grandchildren this may be the most magnificent wildlife experience of their young lives. This is the

"Everglades of the North," the nation's largest freshwater cattail marsh and home to more than 260 species of birds, as well as other animals.

In 1927 the state legislature passed the Horicon Marsh Wildlife Refuge Bill and the southern component was born. In the 1940s, the U.S. Fish and Wildlife Service purchased the northern portion of the marsh and it became a national wildlife refuge. Now the geese are the most dramatic sight and you will see the greatest numbers at dawn and dusk. At midday many leave the marsh to feed in nearby farm fields.

There are a number of ways to explore the marsh. A circular driving route takes you all the way around, with a number of places where you can pull off the main road and get a closer view, including the refuge visitor center and the International Education Center at the Horicon Marsh State Wildlife Area. Main Dike Road cuts through the middle of the marsh and is a good place to stop and use binoculars or a spotting scope to look at the surroundings. The refuge also has a shorter (2.7-mile) auto tour route for a slower, more leisurely view of the wetlands. You can also walk on trails for an even slower, closer look—a 2.5-mile Redhead Hiking Trail and the 1.6-mile Two Hawks Hiking Trail. The third and probably best way to explore the marsh is in a canoe or other shallow draft boat. This will put you in the same habitat with the ducks and geese. Canoes and kayaks can be rented in the town of Horicon and there are public boat ramps in the state wildlife area. You only need to decide which is best for yourself and your grandchildren.

This activity could fill part of one day or a whole weekend, depending on your interests and the weather.

Bonding and bridging:

The Horicon Marsh is the perfect place to talk about learning from our mistakes. Right there in front of you is the example of serious errors in land use. For seventy years one land management mistake followed another. But soon the trees were gone and so was the dam. Today the marsh has been restored and returned to its original state.

We all make mistakes, and the people who grow the most are those who recognize their mistakes and try to do better the next time. Children need to have adults admit that occasionally they've been wrong. This is a great time to let them know that no matter how they might falter they will still be loved. We also need to realize that we are who we are, and trying to be something or someone else is a recipe for disaster. We all need to learn how to live with our strengths and weaknesses.

A word to the wise:

If your grandchild is old enough to paddle a canoe, go to Greenhead Landing on the east side of the state wildlife area and paddle out to see the heron rookery on Fourmile Island. This is a state natural area and the largest nesting colony of great blue herons and great egrets in Wisconsin. (Keep your distance while observing the birds.) You will feel as though you've paddled back in time; the sight and sounds of these large wading birds is almost prehistoric.

Age of grandchild: 8 and up

Best season: Spring (duck migration); fall (Canada goose migration)

Contact:

Horicon Marsh State Wildlife Area, N7725 Highway 28, Horicon, WI 53032 (920) 387-7860 • www.dnr.state.wi.us/ORG/LAND/wildlife/reclands/horicon

Horicon National Wildlife Refuge, W4279 Headquarters Road, Mayville, WI 53050 • (920) 387-2658 • www.fws.gov/midwest/horicon

Also check out:

Necedah National Wildlife Refuge, Necedah: www.fws.gov/midwest/necedah

Trempealeau National Wildlife Refuge, Trempealeau: www.fws.gov/midwest/trempealeau

Grandchildren are God's way of compensating us for growing old. MARY H. WALDRIP

Hartford Balloon Rally

We have balloons for birthdays, we buy balloons at the circus and the zoo, and we use balloons to decorate parties and celebrations. In each occasion the balloon is a symbol of happiness. What is it that we like? Is it the fact that we can capture and control a piece of air? Is it the lightness of its being, the floating, drifting color that is tethered to a string, but which seems to connect us to a mysterious space?

For centuries balloons have been part of flight. Balloons rise and most of the time our spirit rises with them, but in hot air balloons, we actually get aboard and fly with them. It is a celebration of our flight dreams and a lifting of the spirit and body. The big hot air balloons are decorated in wild colors and designs that represent our joy at the experience of lifting off from the Earth.

In Hartford, you and your grandchildren can let your spirits fly in the mass of colorful balloons that take flight each August. Kids from eight to seventeen can take an airplane ride, the first of many—or if not the first flight, the first in a small airplane where you really get a feeling for the sensation of flying.

The balloon liftoff is an early morning event, not for everyone, but worth it for those who can wake in the wee hours to be at the airport when the first rays of the sun come over the horizon. This is a dawn-to-dark experience, and liftoff is the first highlight. But there is a "balloon glow" shortly after dark that competes with the morning takeoff as a memorable moment. The glow is created when the burners fill the balloons with hot air and light, making the inflated globes look like giant Japanese lanterns covered by the rainbow. It is hard to describe the impact of these magnificent giant balloons in the evening and their glowing ascent. Let your imagination soar again with fireworks. The fireworks are worth the length of the day and seem a fitting end for this combination of sky and spirit.

Pace yourself. This event has highs on both ends and a quieter middle. If you feel the need, take a nap. Slow down. Make it fun.

Bonding and bridging:

This event is filled with color and dreams. The dream of flight may have started with the birds and insects, the glow of the moon in the dark night sky, and the invention of kites, but flight itself began with balloons and took us to the moon.

Talk about the wonder of flight and the advances scientists have helped us make. As we understand physics, air and energy, we learn to harness these forces for our use and our entertainment. Help your grandchildren see the dream and let them know that they can have their dreams soar, too, if they study, learn, and apply their knowledge. They may be part of the generation that sets foot on another planet.

A word to the wise:

The Pike Lake Unit of the Kettle Moraine State Forest, near Hartford, includes a section of the Ice Age National Scenic Trail. This is a great opportunity to combine two different experiences—exploring our glacial heritage and our aviation dreams. It is also a good place for camping and swimming. But the hike that connects both experiences is the astronomy trail; walk in nature and explore space!

Age of grandchild: 3 and up

Best season: Summer

Contact: Hartford Area Chamber of Commerce,
225 North Main Street, Hartford, WI 53027
(262) 673-7002 • www.hartfordchamber.org

Also check out:

Hudson Hot Air Affair, Hudson (February): www.hudsonhotairaffair.com

Kettle Moraine State Forest—Pike Lake Unit, Hartford:
www.dnr.state.wi.us/org/land/parks/specific/pikelake

Thunder on the Lakeshore, Manitowoc (June):
www.manitowocairshow.com/balloon.htm

Wausau Balloon Rally & Glow, Wausau (July):
www.wausauballoonrally.com

I've learned that when your newly born grandchild holds your little finger in his fist, that you're hooked for life. Andy Rooney

29

Black Holocaust Museum and the Underground Railroad

The Underground Railroad is not what your grandchildren might expect. No colorful Thomas the Tank engines—this is the route that linked courageous people of all races in the escape from the horror of slavery. Meanwhile, America's Black Holocaust Museum tells the story of the people who had to escape both the institution of slavery and the prejudice of racism. The fact that the terrible injustice of slavery was built into our land of freedom is still hard to grasp, but it is essential that our grandchildren understand it.

Start at America's Black Holocaust Museum where the displays will give you insight into African heritage, courageous activists, slavery, racism and African American culture. The museum can direct your family to sites for Milwaukee's Underground Railroad.

We suggest that you incorporate some of the following historic sites into your exploration of Wisconsin. You have to judge your grandchildren's age and readiness for each of these various sites.

Ripon's Little White Schoolhouse was a combination of Whigs, Northern Democrats and Free Soilers who came together to fight slavery and form the Republican Party.

At the Milwaukee Public Library, the Milwaukee Public Museum and Old World Wisconsin you can learn about the railroad.

Two of the oldest African American churches are in Racine, and the Racine Heritage Museum tells the story.

In Kenosha you can visit the library and take a walking tour to see many homes that housed the fugitive slaves.

The Milton House includes a tunnel connecting the cellar with a back-lot cabin used for storage and a place to hide the escapees.

Eau Claire's Carson Park hosts a statue of baseball great Hank Aaron, who broke into segregated baseball when he played on the city's minor league team.

Slavery is a complex and confusing story because it makes no sense and we cannot see how it ever did. Be prepared for your grandchildren to have some discomfort with what you are seeing, and use that for conversation.

Bonding and bridging:

At times we suggest activities that are interesting, but not filled with laughter and lightness. Our grandchildren must learn about the world, the injustices as well as justice. You need to help them get grounded in values they will live by and will demand from our nation and other people.

Change is difficult and people sometimes pay great prices for speaking up, but our country has a history of courageous people who questioned slavery, Indian treatment, destruction of the environment, and fighting unnecessary wars. Your grandchildren have the potential to make a difference. This is one of the areas where you can help them to see their own potential for good.

A word to the wise:

In *Grandparents Wisconsin Style* we suggest visiting Norwegian and Swiss settlements. We celebrate ethnicity in community festivals. You might ask why there are no African American festivals. There is only one community in Wisconsin founded by African Americans—Lake Ivanhoe. Slaves could not found communities; they could not bring their celebrations and heritage. This is part of the tragedy of racism.

Age of grandchild: 10 and up

Best season: All

Contact: America's Black Holocaust Museum, 2233 North 4th Street, Milwaukee, WI 53212 • (414) 264-2500 • www.blackholocaustmuseum.org

Also check out:

The Milton House Museum, Milton: www.miltonhouse.org

Old World Wisconsin, Eagle: www.wisconsinhistory.org/oww

Racine Heritage Museum, Racine: www.racineheritagemuseum.org

Children's Museums

Is this a museum or a playground? Does it matter? To the kids it is their place. There are several floors of creativity. Color, design and educational content are interwoven into one of the most child-engaging places possible. It is the job of the grandparent to guide them through, letting the child's imagination make the choices, while you watch over safety and the possible conflict from lots of little hands and feet concentrating on the objects that have grabbed their attention and not on who else is grabbing, where people are walking, and who is crawling.

This is creative play; imagination is the real tool in the experience, and it can lead to creative thinking, problem solving and intuitive response in later life. The grandparents need to suspend their reality and engage in the minds of the grandchildren. Don't worry if they get wet in the water areas—bring extra clothes. Sometimes it is necessary to cajole and make sure that there is sharing, but don't turn into a bully even on behalf of your grandchildren. Let the children learn how to play together, as well as fantasize in the world constructed by each display.

Wisconsin has some exceptional children's museums and we recommend both the Betty Brinn Children's Museum in Milwaukee and the Madison Children's Museum because of the imaginative settings they have created. That said, all of the children's museums in the state have something special to offer. Take advantage of them as you travel or seek experiences for your grandchild.

Think about the way children try to emulate adults. Here they are encouraged to act out the roles they have created in their minds. They are offered adult settings but not told how to fulfill the roles they choose. Whether it is a dairy farm, a market or a TV studio—the story is theirs to create. As a supervising adult, allow them this freedom and do not impose your ideas—instead, observe, enjoy and learn.

Many museums see the role of grandparents as essential to the child and offer a season pass at the same rate paid by the parents. These passes often are accepted at other children's museums as well. It is a very good deal!

Bonding and bridging:

In play, the child looks for approval, and grandparents are ideal candidates to encourage, praise and offer some new insights. It is an important role and grandparents need to allow the children to have the experience—that means stepping back and letting them explore. It means not reaching in and competing with children for the balls and boats and materials—but rather, letting grandchildren know how to get things for themselves.

Use the reading area and the lunch breaks and the ride home to talk about what they liked. Help them learn to pace themselves (a very tough task) and process the things they learn. "How did that .... work?" "What did you like best? Why?"

A word to the wise:

This is your day to enable and observe. Take advantage of programs where the staff helps children create objects, using art and focusing their energies and enthusiasm. This is a good slow-down place that still engages the child fully. And when it feels overwhelming, let the children know that Grandpa or Grandma is a little tired and if they will go to one of the quiet areas with you and relax with you awhile, they can stay even longer.

Age of grandchild: Up to age 10

Best season: All

Contact:

Betty Brinn Children's Museum, 929 East Wisconsin Avenue, Milwaukee, WI 53202 • (414) 390-5437 • www.bbcmkids.org

Madison Children's Museum, 100 State Street, Madison, WI 53703 (608) 256-6445 • www.madisonchildrensmuseum.org

Also check out:

The Building for Kids, Appleton: www.kidmuseum.org

Central Wisconsin Children's Museum, Stevens Point: www.cwchildrensmuseum.org

Children's Museum of La Crosse, La Crosse: www.childmuseumlax.org

At age seven, children have as passionate a longing for creative interactions and learning as they earlier had for explorations of the world. Joseph Chilton Pearce, *The Magical Child*

Discovery World

We went looking for things our grandchildren should discover and learn and came away learning things that we grandparents need to know. If you are passive you can watch everyone else have fun, but that's not what the newest of Milwaukee's lakefront museums is all about. Here is a day of doing!

Discovery World came into existence in 2006 because of Michael Cudahy, Wisconsin businessman-philanthropist who believed that the old Discovery World and Pier Wisconsin could be combined. He said, "I saw kids going in one door sort of 'blah' and coming out the other excited, with sparkles in their eyes. They were going to be astronauts or doctors or scientists. If we could do that with several hundred kids a year and we batted ten percent, think how many lives we could change for the better!"

Start with the exciting structure called the Technology Building. You enter through a gleaming glass-walled promenade that opens onto 450 feet of public docks along Lake Michigan. Inside there are dozens of exhibits including a massive double-helix staircase that follows a forty-foot model of a human genome that can be programmed to move to music and color. In the Rockwell Dream Machine you and your grandchildren can produce things like a miniature of the *Denis Sullivan* schooner that sails from the museum during the summer as a floating museum program.

In a separate but attached circular building designed to look like a Great Lakes schooner pilothouse, the Reiman Family Aquariums bring the world that the *Sullivan* travels inside. Upstairs is a full-scale model of the wooden schooner that allows you to walk the deck, turn the wheel and explore the 1850 seaman's world. On the first floor is a forty-by-forty-foot scale model of the Great Lakes. The model even lets you create and observe storms.

Below the ship and the map is our favorite—the aquariums that trace the freshwater and saltwater habitats found during the Milwaukee-to-the-Caribbean voyage of the *Denis Sullivan*. The tanks are set up so you walk over the fish, beside the fish and occasionally under the fish.

The result is learning at its best.

Bonding and bridging:

This fast-paced museum honors the past, the present and the possible. It's a place where we find the magic in discovery and the creativity of the human mind. Maybe this is a good place to talk to your grandchildren about the discoveries that have happened in your lifetime, and they can gain some insight into the rapid change that will surround their lives.

What do they think will be discovered and in place when they reach your age? What are the changes they expect soon? Can they imagine the world as we grew up? Can they understand that we did not know what a computer in the home would be? You can share with them that the original computers would have filled a home. But the main point is to bring your lives together through discovery.

A word to the wise:

This is a new facility and since they are focused on discovery, the museum will change regularly. Use that as the theme. Give yourself a few hours and go to one part of the museum. Get engaged, have lunch and reflect, then decide to come back or go on, based on your energy level. Make the morning and the afternoon of a day visit completely different. Enjoy the high-tech areas in the morning and contrast them with the boat and the aquarium in the afternoon.

Age of grandchild: 5 and up

Best season: All

Contact: Discovery World, 500 North Harbor Drive, Milwaukee, WI 53202 • (414) 765-9966 • www.discoveryworld.org

Also check out:

Milwaukee Public Museum, Milwaukee: www.mpm.edu

University of Wisconsin—Madison Geology Museum, Madison: www.geology.wisc.edu/~museum

Weis Earth Science Museum, Menasha: www.uwfox.uwc.edu/wesm

Wisconsin Maritime Museum, Manitowoc: www.wisconsinmaritime.org

Lake Michigan Ferry Ride

Lake Michigan forms one border of the state, but it is also something of a roadblock. Traveling to Michigan means traveling around the lake and that takes a lot of time (especially if you have to go through Chicago), but there is another option. You could just hop on a ferry and go across the lake.

We do not have a culture of cruise boats on the Great Lakes, but we have a wonderful history of working boats and your grandchildren have heard about

pirates, explorers and sailors. They know the romance of the sea in film and story, so how about giving them a little sea time yourself on the ferry?

The *Lake Express* runs from Milwaukee to Muskegon in only 2½ hours, each way. It is a modern high-speed ferry with seats inside and out. A longer option (four hours) is the *S.S. Badger*, which connects Manitowoc, Wisconsin, and Ludington, Michigan.

Think about how this adventure feels for your grandchildren. They will be excited by the boat and the sailing. They will want to explore the boat when you first get on and they will watch as you pull away from the dock. Point out the gulls and the details! Help them find things to focus on. Then as the ship moves out of port be ready for relaxation—isn't that what a cruise is for?

Bring some food or buy from the on-board cafeteria. Have a book to read, maybe a puzzle, a board game and binoculars.

The *Badger* has a movie theater and this is not a bad option for part of the cruise since the round trip would be eight hours. There is also a KidsPort play area for younger children.

On the high-speed ferry, you can add to the adventure by contrasting the large city—Milwaukee and all its options—with Muskegon, the beach town in Michigan. If you go from Manitowoc, you should walk the harbor, and in Ludington take advantage of great hikes in the dunes and parks.

Bring your car if you want a longer stay or want to make a round trip that includes both ferries, but it is not necessary if you are just looking for a boat ride. Bicycles are a cheaper and healthier option.

Bonding and bridging:

The time that you are just floating is good for reading, resting and playing, but it is also time for personal sharing. Think of how the world now belongs to you and your grandchildren. For the duration of the ride there is nothing you have to do. You have no place to go, no phone calls to make. How often does that happen? Enjoy the chance to get refreshed. Ask your grandchildren what makes them feel good. What makes them happy? If they are old enough, talk about what makes them feel relaxed.

Relaxation is something Americans lose. Hinduism and Buddhism have significant rituals and beliefs that center on the ability to relax and meditate. Ask the children what makes them laugh and smile.

A word to the wise:

The story of the Great Lakes is a story of boats, and one of the best things you can do to enhance your trip is visit the Rogers Street Fishing Village and Great Lakes Coast Guard Museum on the East Twin River. This area had a history of more than 165 years starting in 1837 and includes an 1886 lighthouse and a new exhibit on commercial fishing. This great historical location will have more meaning as you begin your own Great Lakes adventure.

Age of grandchild: 3 and up

Best season: Summer

Contact:

Lake Express, 2330 South Lincoln Memorial Drive, Milwaukee, WI 53207 • (866) 914-1010 • www.lake-express.com

Lake Michigan Carferry, 701 Maritime Drive, Ludington, MI 49431 (800) 841-4243 • www.ssbadger.com

Also check out:

Cassville Car Ferry, Cassville: www.cassville.org/ferry.html

Washington Island Ferry Line, Washington Island: www.wisferry.com

They say genes skip generations. Maybe that's why grandparents find their grandchildren so likeable. Joan McIntosh

37

Milwaukee Art Museum

What are the differences between art and nonsense? It is not easy to define art. What makes a painting valuable—is it the willingness of another person to pay for it, or is there some measure that the art world has? There are no easy answers to these questions, but there is no doubt that art has an important place in our lives. We collect it, we use it for advertising and we hang it on our walls. So maybe the best approach for grandparents and grandchildren is to just explore the world of art and see what attracts you.

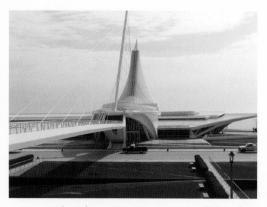

A visit to the Milwaukee Art Museum begins with the building called the Quadracci Pavillion, designed by Santiago Calatrava. We prefer to start at the Betty Brinn Children's Museum and walk across the Reiman pedestrian bridge. There are many views from the plaza before you cross over the road. Take a look and see if you can spot a ship. The second experience is entering the expansive open area beneath the sail of the building and enjoying the view through the wall of windows. Already your perspective will be changed, and that is what art is all about. Ask your grandchildren about their impressions and their perspective as you go.

The art museum has been in existence since 1888, but in different locations and with different names. This building was created in 2001 and has become a destination for locals and visitors alike, located on the Lake Michigan shoreline and near many other attractions.

The museum recommends a game plan before coming. There is too much to see in one visit and the best parts of such a visit come from staying with the children's interests and energy levels. You can always return for an adult visit. The exhibits include photography, painting, sculpture, glass and ceramics. Look at a few items in each until you find an area that captures the children's imagination—this is a discovery trip, not an art class!

One of our favorite pieces is by Duane Hanson, a sculpture so lifelike it will make you wonder if it is a real person posing. This is a fun place to take photos of your grandchildren interacting with art.

Bonding and bridging:

Why do we like art? Ask your grandchildren why they like drawing and coloring. That is the beginning of art. Do they enjoy making things, playing with clay, building sand castles?

Talk about what you like and why, ask them what they like best. Maybe you can pick up a children's book on art in the museum store and use that for your conversation. They have some great ones, such as *The Museum ABC* and *The Museum Shapes in Art*—both from the Metropolitan Museum of Art.

Finally, with art in mind, a few crayons or some paints might just be the perfect way to let the pent-up artistic expression loose. If creating art is fun, it will mean even more to them.

A word to the wise:

The museum website recommends the following to families and we think it is good advice:

Be realistic about your family's stamina levels; a four-hour visit may not be a good idea. Better to have a great two-hour visit and leave happy.

Consider your children's schedule for naptime or quiet time when planning the time of day to visit.

Plan for a rest or snack break during your visit. A little fresh air, a bit of juice, or just a chance to sit down makes for a more comfortable trip.

Age of grandchild: 5 and up

Best season: All

Contact: Milwaukee Art Museum, 700 North Art Museum Drive, Milwaukee, WI 53202 • (414) 224-3200 • www.mam.org

Also check out:

Bergstrom-Mahler Museum, Neenah: www.bergstrom-mahlermuseum.com

Chazen Museum of Art, Madison: www.chazen.wisc.edu

John Michael Kohler Arts Center, Sheboygan: www.jmkac.org

Milwaukee Public Museum

The Milwaukee Public Museum has a solid, stoic look on the outside, but that belies the fun inside the doors. Unique among museums, this one was set up without the help of philanthropists and was always intended to be a "people's museum." Its collections grew out of student field trips to local areas, as well as donations from folks who traveled to foreign lands and contributed objects of scientific and historic interest.

Like most other natural and human history museums, there is more to see than a person—young or old—can absorb in one visit. Better to make this a

place you come back to regularly, adding new sections each time. Your grandchildren, as they grow older, will have new and different interests anyway. The museum includes exhibits with lifelike people and animals from Asia, the Arctic, Africa, the Oceans, South and Middle America, the Pacific Islands and even a rain forest. These exhibits alone cover 150,000 square feet.

Probably one of the most fascinating exhibits is the Puelicher Butterfly Wing. In this two-story space, butterflies of all colors and sizes flutter around, sometimes landing on visitors' fingers. What better place to escape a case of winter cabin fever than this garden filled with exotic and magical life? Right next to this is a learning gallery where you and the kids can get involved with interactive stations and a larger-than-life habitat, complete with costumes that let them become caterpillars and butterflies.

Other spots that will intrigue and delight are the European Village with child-size homes that you can peer into, and the Streets of Old Milwaukee. Finally, knowing the popularity of dinosaurs, don't miss the Third Planet, which includes a *T. Rex* towering in all its glory.

If you buy a membership to the museum, one of the benefits is something called the Clue Crew Kids Club. Any time you come with the grandchildren, they can pick up a Clue Crew case sheet, which turns them into detectives, as they look for answers to the questions on the sheets. This can help create a focus to each visit. There are currently forty different case sheets.

Bonding and bridging:

History. How many of us remember yawning in class or daydreaming when that subject came up? This generation of grandchildren is no different than we were, but a good museum can create excitement and curiosity about the past that the classroom never can.

Every one of us has a personal history, and when it's personal, it is always more interesting. Talk with your grandchildren about events that have been important to them. Was it the first day of school, the holidays, the house that they moved to? Then tell them some of the important parts of your history, but not so many that their eyes glaze over. If they're old enough, this would be a good time to show them an example of a family tree, with a photo album of pictures of ancestors. Sometimes we can see resemblances to people who lived long before us.

A word to the wise:

Bugs Alive! There are so many fun and interesting exhibits at the museum, it's hard to know where to start, but if you have a grandchild interested in insects, you must visit this newer exhibit. These are species that they won't ever find at home or in their yards—exotic and extremely important to the health of the planet. If you're not crazy about bugs, this may be a time to push beyond your comfort zone for your grandchild's sake. You might even come away with a different opinion about bugs. There is an opportunity for hands-on activities at midday, depending on the availability of volunteer staff.

Age of grandchild: 3 and up

Best season: All

Contact: Milwaukee Public Museum, 800 West Wells Street, Milwaukee, WI 53233 • (414) 278-2702 • www.mpm.edu

Also check out:

Kenosha Public Museum, Kenosha: www.kenosha.org/departments/museum

Neville Public Museum, Green Bay: www.nevillepublicmuseum.org

Oshkosh Public Museum, Oshkosh: www.oshkoshmuseum.org

Now that I've reached the age where I need my children more than they need me, I really understand how grand it is to be a grandmother. Mrs. Margaret Whitlam

Mitchell Park Conservatory

We have a love affair with plants. Think of all the nurseries and greenhouse businesses in the world! How many homes are without at least one flower? And who does not miss a touch of green in a Wisconsin February?

Early explorers included people like Joseph Banks, who sailed with James Cook and had the task of bringing new and exotic plants to the collectors of the western world. Marco Polo journeyed across continents looking for spices, and those same spices were in the dreams of Christopher Columbus, Magellan and other historic wanderers. In fact, spices were more a factor than gold in many of these explorations. But while we sought treasure, we also sought pleasure and the works of the naturalist were displayed in famous places like the Royal Botanical Gardens in England, Le Jardin des Plantes in Paris, or Hortus Botanicus at the University of Leiden, Holland.

Luckily, the Mitchell Park Conservatory is a place where grandparents and grandchildren can still search for exotic spices in the air and beautiful greenery exuding oxygen and a feeling of warmth and summer. The domes are the only structure of their kind in the world. The Milwaukee Conservatory was built in 1898 and lasted until 1955, when costs of repair and upkeep made it

impractical. It was replaced with Donald Grieb's three beehive-shaped glass domes, which were completed in 1967.

Now you and your grandchildren can take an exotic trip without leaving the comfort of the domes. Wander the rain forest, feel the dampness and look for hidden flowers among the large green leaves. Then if you are feeling too damp and want to dry off, walk to the desert biome, where cacti and yucca and other dry-land plants give you a feeling for the world of monitor lizards and desert tortoises. Each dome is a unique experience, with paths and benches to help you relax and take in the experience. They are also good places to sit and watch birds that make these unique habitats home.

If exotic travel is not on your itinerary, enjoy the Floral Show Dome where you will find a wonderful array of flowers that might be blooming later in your neighborhood gardens. This is a playland setting that is comfortable in both temperature and familiarity.

Bonding and bridging:

Want to take a trip with your grandchildren to a tropical locale? Imagination is your ticket. Get out the globe, look at the world between the Tropic of Cancer and the Tropic of Capricorn (already sounds exotic!). Your imaginary trip will be to a land of deserts and rain forests, a zone of fantastic countries, where the people speak new languages and have new ways to live. Help your grandchildren understand how different it must be for people living in other places and how hard it must be for them to understand us.

Print yourselves a ticket and take that trip. Budget is hardly a concern for travelers with imagination. Bring along a daypack with water to drink (you are going to the hot climates), a camera or notepad—always keep notes of your trip—and maybe you can send a note to your friends in faraway Wisconsin.

A word to the wise:

They have many special programs during the year and you should check the schedule. These are three of our favorites from past programming: (1.) This Land Is Your Land is a model railroad show that combines small plants with the railroads. (2.) Whimsical Garden matches art and sculpture with the natural nooks and crannies of the garden. (3.) Rainforest Night is a night in the jungle. Use your flashlights and have a wonderful experience in the dark.

Age of grandchild: All

Best season: All

Contact: Mitchell Park Conservatory,
524 South Layton Boulevard, Milwaukee, WI 53215
(414) 649-9800 • www.county.milwaukee.gov

Also check out:

Boerner Botanical Gardens, Hales Corners: www.boernerbotanicalgardens.org

Green Bay Botanical Garden, Green Bay: www.gbbg.org

Olbrich Botanical Gardens, Madison: www.ci.madison.wi.us/olbrich

Schlitz Audubon Nature Center

Want to get out of Milwaukee but not too far? Want to explore the natural landscape of Lake Michigan without making your grandchildren spend too much time in the car? Would you like to find a place where the buildings are the best of green architecture and still find the kinds of trails that give you good exercise, bird watching and wildflowers? If so, Schlitz Audubon Center is one of the premier destinations in the country.

The center is designed to accommodate—schools, scouts and clubs—but don't let that keep you from walking and searching the grounds and building.

There are places to sit and explore inside the building and there are hikes and programs by professional educators that will enthrall your grandchildren.

True to Milwaukee's history, this was once the land of a great brewer. Joseph Schlitz acquired 185 acres in 1885 and the site became a family recreational area. Luckily the ravines, bluffs and shoreline were saved. Dorothy Vallier worked for nine years to make this a National Audubon Center and showed a remarkable persistence that is rewarded by the sanctuary now available to your family.

Six miles of trails deserve your time and attention. Hiking for exercise is good, but exercising the mind as well as the body is the perfect blend for a two- or three-hour hike with your grandchildren. Hiking gives you the sense of the landscape and while on the hike you can let loose your senses. Take in the scent of spring and summer flowers, listen to the roar of the waves and the calls of the birds, feel the texture of the trail surface, feel the webs of erstwhile spiders seeking their living along the paths, and take in the colors of the leaves, the waters, the flowers and the soil.

Come regularly. Come in sun and cloud, in calm and in wind. You'll see the variations in the water texture and tint, just as you observe the changes in green throughout the growing season and the burst of color in the fall.

The value of this place just six miles from downtown Milwaukee is that you can get to it often and in the repeat visits you make connections between your observations and the complex cycles of nature.

Bonding and bridging:

The Schlitz Audubon Nature Center's mission is "connect people with nature and inspire them to become responsible stewards of the natural world," but it could also include connecting people to the natural world. There is no better place for bonding and bridging, whether it is at the lakeshore throwing rocks, catching the coolness of a summer breeze, watching the birds at the feeder, or helping one another down the steep path.

In a location like this we lose the trappings of school, work and home, and we just are who we are. One study determined that ninety-five percent of a person's learning takes place outside the formal school setting. In this setting we can explore our values and connect.

A word to the wise:

Taking a rest after climbing the lookout or walking up from the beach is a good idea. The center has a good option on the deck—with comfortable benches that make it possible to rest and relax while continuing to take in the scenery. There is plenty of space for the kids if they are still full of energy, and you can decompress before getting back in your car and heading out of this wonderful setting.

Age of grandchild: All

Best season: Spring

Contact: Schlitz Audubon Nature Center, 1111 East Brown Deer Road, Milwaukee, WI 53217 • (414) 352-2880 • www.schlitzauduboncenter.com

Also check out:

Mosquito Hill Nature Center, New London:
www.co.outagamie.wi.us/Parks/MH_home.htm

River Bend Nature Center, Racine:
www.explorewisconsin.com/countypages/racine.html

Riveredge Nature Center, Newburg: www.riveredgenaturecenter.org

Woodland Dunes Nature Center, Two Rivers: www.woodlanddunes.com

There is no other door to knowledge than the door Nature opens. And there is no truth but the truth we discover in Nature. LUTHER BURBANK

Bristol Renaissance Faire

Knights, pirates, swordsmen and Robin Hood make the Renaissance Faire an event for great imagination and theatrics. The setting is an ancient European city where knights wore armor, carried the colors of their allegiance and lived for honor.

On the other extreme we have the pirates, perhaps the most despicable of our colorful historic characters. Imagine these rough characters of legend as your

gruff companions in this imaginary landscape. The Renaissance Faire is also filled with magicians, minstrels, storytellers and artisans. Wander among all these characters with your grandchildren in a wonderful make-believe with a historic origin.

The day includes theatrical productions, dramatic jousting contests, puppets and characters of legend and fable. Even Queen Elizabeth I appears at the event to knight the courageous and to address all the women in waiting. Look for the magical Fantastikals troupe of fairies and sprites near the Dirty Duck Inn.

But you must engage in the make-believe if you and your grandchildren are to get the most out of this activity. Suspend your rational mind and get into the time of the Renaissance, accept the characters as real and allow the events of the day to happen without twenty-first century skepticism. You are here to enjoy, not to judge.

Young children will want to go to Kids Kingdom where Hansel and Gretel, Little Red Riding Hood, Cinderella and other fairy tale characters wander and the rides are geared for the youngest. Then they can explore a pirate ship. Older grandchildren will want to see the knights and armor.

But whatever your plans, make sure you watch the midday royal parade. This will introduce your family to the variety of characters and costumes that create the spice and pageant of the Faire.

Bonding and bridging:

The history of the world is a variety of stories. Here history is romanticized and fun, but some of these characters, like the pirates, really weren't admirable people. It would be good to talk about that. Talk about why gunslingers, pirates and gangsters are considered colorful and are the subjects of story and movies. Would you want them as your neighbors? What is the difference between colorful and valuable? Who are the people in our lives who are really significant? Why aren't they the subjects of stories and legend? Why don't we have stories about grandparents? You can have some fun exploring these questions.

A word to the wise:

Why do we enjoy costumes? Halloween would not be half the fun if it didn't include dressing up in costumes. Renaissance fairs are costume events and they trigger our imagination. If you can come in costume, you will have even more fun. Help your grandchildren get into the mood by making a costume that will really make them a part of the event. We've set aside clothing from the various decades that we have lived through and now those too will be great fun for the grandchildren to dress up in and drift off into make-believe.

Age of grandchild: 4 and up

Best season: July through Labor Day

Contact: Bristol Renaissance Faire, 12550 120th Avenue, Kenosha, WI 53142 • (847) 395-7773 • www.recfair.com/bristol

Also check out:

Janesville Renaissance Faire, Janesville: www.jvlfaire.gsmbristol.org

Ren Fest, Wausau: www.renaissancefestival.com/viewEvent.asp?eventID=324

Wisconsin Renaissance Fair, Chippewa Falls: www.wirenfaire.com

Old World Wisconsin

We can talk all we want about the old times, when people had to work long hours in the fields and kids had to walk miles to school, but for our grandchildren, that's probably about as interesting as watching C-Span. Old World Wisconsin brings "ancient" history to life, with real live people acting out the parts of the early Wisconsin settlers.

Spread over 576 acres of wooded hills and prairie in the southern unit of the Kettle Moraine State Forest, this living history site is the largest in the

Midwest. There are ten farmsteads clustered in small enclaves of ethnic groups, much as they would have been in the past. You can visit German, Polish, Finnish, Danish, Norwegian and African American communities, plus a village that features businesses typically found in the 1870s. The buildings have been moved from other locations around the state, but they are all original structures.

Throughout the season and on special days during the "off-season" visitors can take part in programs that are more theater than history lessons. What better way to learn than to witness a temperance rally (with hymn singing and testimonials from reformed drinkers) or Town Hall debates, based on actual debates from more than a century ago?

There are live animals at the various homesteads, and you can get close to baby animals at Caldwell Farmers' Club Hall. Other daily events throughout the outdoor museum include appearances by the local tax assessor and the Wisconsin gubernatorial candidate, "Fighting" Bob La Follette. Craftspeople are on hand to demonstrate skills long gone, such as blacksmithing, spinning, flax processing, wood-stove cooking and hundreds of other daily tasks.

When you arrive you can pick up an activity book for the kids that includes clues and things to look for as you tour the site. A motorized tram can take you around to the various homesteads, but we recommend walking between some of them—if for no other reason than to give the grandkids a sense of what it was like to wander country roads, scuffing rocks along the way.

Restaurant food is available in the Clausing Barn, but why not make it a more authentic visit and pack a picnic lunch in an old-fashioned wicker basket?

Bonding and bridging:

If your grandchildren are in grade school or older they have probably heard their parents or other adults talk about immigration and immigrants. It is a hot-button topic now, but here you are at a place that celebrates our immigrant heritage. Talk to the grandkids about their ancestry—where their great-great-grandparents came from. Ask them what it would feel like to leave their home and all that they knew to travel thousands of miles to a place unlike anything they knew before. We are a country created from diversity and our culture is richer because of all those who have brought pieces of the old country with them. It's still happening today, though the people are coming from different continents. Ask the grandchildren if they know kids in school who have come from other countries. Thinking about the difficulties of coming to a new land as someone in their family once did may give them reason to empathize with the new immigrants.

A word to the wise:

What is really great about Old World Wisconsin is the number and variety of special events that go on throughout the year. Just a few examples include Rituals of Spring, with real sheep shearing; Baseball History Day in June—complete with a vintage team; Swedish Midsommar Celebration; Morgan Horse Day; Old World Wedding; and Autumn Lamplight Tours—just to name a few. But probably the best one to attend with the grandkids is Laura Ingalls Wilder Day in August. This is a day when the kids can dress up in old-fashioned clothes and take part in a look-a-like contest and an old-fashioned spelling bee. The theme for the day is based on the author's book *Farmer Boy*.

Age of grandchild: 9 and up

Best season: Late spring through early fall

Contact: Old World Wisconsin, S103 W37890 Highway 67, Eagle, WI 53119 • (262) 594-6300 • www.wisconsinhistory.org/oww

Also check out:

Pendarvis, Mineral Point: www.wisconsinhistory.org/pendarvis

Stonefield, Cassville: www.wisconsinhistory.org/stonefield

Dane County Farmers' Market

Maybe you've had the good fortune to travel to Europe and wander through the colorful, lively and fascinating outdoor markets. It is a social occasion where friends and neighbors meet and chat, and children chase one another around the legs of adults.

I was lucky to have a grandmother who had been a farmer, so a weekly trip to the farmers' market was her way to keep that part of her past alive. There were

many Saturday mornings when I was roused from my bed to accompany my mother and grandmother to the market. Any grumpiness I felt was erased as soon as I smelled the ripe cantaloupe. Memories of those Saturday mornings with her, among the multi-colored and sensuous smells of the Earth's bounty, are some of the best I have.

Farmers' markets exist all over Wisconsin, but the *crème de la crème* is in Madison and is known as the Dane County Farmers' Market. Established in 1972, this market has close to three hundred vendors who come on Wednesdays and Saturdays to set up their displays around Capitol Square. This market is reportedly the largest producer-only farmers' market in the country, and all agriculturally related items must be produced in Wisconsin.

Very few children have the experience of caring for animals, picking food for the evening meal or even running free in the pasture. A farmers' market with its colorful tables of produce, flowers, meats and baked goods may be as close as many children will get to being at a farm or meeting a farmer.

Go early and wander leisurely. There is music across the street, sometimes samples to nibble and great people watching. The smells, sounds, textures and colors are images that will stay with your grandchild.

There are so many lessons in this visit. Think about the contrasts between a farmers' market and a supermarket, such as the packaging (or lack thereof). Also consider what healthy food is and what the word "organic" means. At the farmers' market you can ask these questions of the people selling their fruits and vegetables. They may not be able to answer every question, but they can fill in a lot of the unknowns about the foods we eat.

Bonding and bridging:

It's easy to take food for granted. Whenever we want it, we know where to get it. A simple trip to the grocery store takes care of our needs. Rarely do we consider the question, "Where does this food come from?"

A farmers' market is a chance to open your grandchildren's eyes to the hard work and dedication that go into everything we eat. They can meet some of the people who work tirelessly to provide us with food.

Tell them how important farmers are to our way of life. Share with them how difficult growing crops truly is and how we would struggle if there were no farmers to do this job. For older children, you may also want to bring up third-world countries in which food supplies are scarce. Either way, this is definitely a time when you want to help your grandchildren learn to appreciate every meal.

A word to the wise:

Ask your grandchildren to think about what they'd like to have for lunch, and make your visit one of finding the best ingredients—it can become a treasure hunt. Even the pickiest eater probably likes tomatoes, corn on the cob or watermelon. To complete the morning's excursion, let your grandchildren choose a bouquet of freshly cut flowers to put on the table during the meal.

Age of grandchild: All

Best season: Late spring through early fall

Contact: Dane County Farmers' Market, PO Box 1485, Madison, WI 53701 • (608) 455-1999 • www.madfarmmkt.org

Also check out:

A listing of Wisconsin farmers' markets: www.wisconline.com/attractions/farmmarkets.html

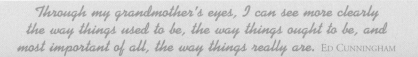

Through my grandmother's eyes, I can see more clearly the way things used to be, the way things ought to be, and most important of all, the way things really are. ED CUNNINGHAM

University of Wisconsin— Madison Geology Museum

Would you own a house without a foundation? Would you live in a home where you never went into the basement? For all of us and for all of Earth, geology is the science that explains our basement. It tells us if there are cracks we have to worry about, if the furnace is too hot, if there is water we can use or water that will seep in where we do not want it. This is where we store things and sometimes find unexpected surprises.

The University of Wisconsin–Madison Geology Museum is open to the public and is filled with fun for grandparents and grandchildren. Tell them that you are going to the basement to see what treasures you might find. The museum has things ready for fun and learning. You will touch rocks from ancient eras, find fossils of creatures that swam where you are walking, and walk around and beneath ancient ice age mammals like the mastodon.

If you are a rock collector, the section on rocks and minerals will inspire you to look closer at the rocks in quarries, beaches and gravel pits. But even if you do not collect rocks, you will enjoy the eerie glow of the minerals in the black-light display. These fluorescent minerals hide their vibrant colors in normal sunlight but absorb the ultraviolet light we call black light. The electrons take the light energy and get energized themselves, so much so that they glow and give off heat and crazy colors in the display. Look at your clothing, too; it will look much different in this light.

As you leave this dazzling display, your path will take you through a small, reconstructed cave where you can see the strange structures of this underground cavity.

To expand your horizons even more, there are extraterrestrial rocks in the display. That's right: visitors from outer space. We call them meteorites and the Geology Museum has a wonderful collection of these rocks that dropped from the sky.

The Earth is full of stories and some people have made it their careers to read and understand them. With the help of the museum, you can help your grandchildren learn that every rock they pick up is connected to the history of the world.

Bonding and bridging:

Getting children to observe the world around them is a key to their future success and this museum provides excellent resources to focus their observations. Go to their website and look at the self-guided tour book in the education section. It contains wonderful background information written in a very clear way, plus it has little questions with a Sherlock Holmes icon: "Can you find three green minerals in exhibit 3?" Then go to the scavenger hunts and select the one for your grandchild's age.

The website changes the way you explore the museum. Many people are passive observers and are lucky if they retain anything they see. But active learning is what you want to encourage in your grandchildren. The scavenger hunt makes all of you look closer. It is observation, discovery and reward. Try it out, but let them do most of the finding. As they grow, this ability will serve them well.

A word to the wise:

Check out the University's "Science Expeditions" event in March. It is open to the public and is family-friendly. The event encompasses the geology museum, the Ingersoll Physics Museum, primate center learning lobby, botany greenhouse and gardens, and the engineering building. There are hands-on experiments and learning opportunities throughout the campus. This expo is perfect to introduce your grandchildren to the world of science and the careers they might want when they grow up.

Age of grandchild: 8 and up

Best season: Early fall through early summer

Contact: University of Wisconsin–Madison Geology Museum,
1215 West Dayton Street, Madison, WI 53706
(608) 262-2399 • www.geology.wisc.edu/~museum

Also check out:

University of Wisconsin–Madison "Science on Campus," Madison: www.science.wisc.edu

Weis Earth Science Museum, Menasha: www.uwfox.uwc.edu/wesm

Elephants and grandchildren never forget. ANDY ROONEY

Henry Vilas Zoo

Around 5,000 years ago in Egypt, where human culture had developed cities, writing and the first empires, were the first zoos. These were strictly for the entertainment and curiosity of the ruling classes—another way to demonstrate wealth and power. Five hundred years later, the first zoo in China was founded by Emperor Wen Wang. The Greeks and Romans also kept private zoos.

By the time zoos began to show up in Europe, many had shrunk to what became known as menageries—small collections of a few species kept in abysmal conditions. In 1907, a German animal dealer and zoo owner named Carl Hagenback developed a new way of exhibiting animals—using a moat. This new style of exhibit gradually spread around the world and can still be found today in almost all zoos. It dramatically improved the life of zoo animals and the experience for visitors.

In the last half of the twentieth century, another sea change in the zoo world took place. The concept of zoos as strictly entertainment facilities was replaced with an understanding that the animals were ambassadors from the wild, that they could educate as well as entertain us and that we may even be more responsible for them now with the loss of habitat around the world. So were born conservation and breeding programs in zoos.

We humans have not lost our fascination with watching other creatures, and children seem to be especially enraptured by all things that creep, crawl, fly and swim. At fourteen months old, our grandson Ryan, who could barely see over the concrete wall, became captivated by the sight of giraffes. He had not even seen a picture of one, but we could barely peel him away from this exhibit.

Modern zoos come in all sizes, but bigger is not always better. While the Milwaukee County Zoo is the largest in the state and has the most extensive collection of animals, we highly recommend the Henry Vilas Zoo in Madison. This zoo is free to the public, easily walked in a couple hours, and is working hard to upgrade its animal exhibits.

Bonding and bridging:

The excitement of the children seeing these new, living creatures is contagious and you will remember the same thrill you felt the first time you saw a lion or a giraffe. We are all fascinated by animals, especially those we rarely see. Here are animals known to be dangerous to humans, but we can watch them from a safe distance and marvel at their grace and beauty.

"Funny," "scary" and "amazing" are all words that describe the sights in a zoo; they can provide a prompt discussion as you wander from exhibit to exhibit. The zoo also gives us a chance to talk about nature and the animals that live in the wild. Why are some endangered? And what can we do to help them survive? You may get into a discussion with an older child about the more difficult questions/issues of captivity. Is it right? If so, why? Kids really do empathize with animals. They want to be good caretakers and we grandparents should nurture that empathy.

A word to the wise:

The primate exhibit at the Henry Vilas Zoo is one of the best we've seen. There are only three exhibits, but the animals are in realistic surroundings and great emphasis is given to the crisis facing primates worldwide. These animals are our closest relatives and as good stewards of the planet we need to know and care about their fate. Quiet is encouraged as you walk into the building and in front of each exhibit, so this may not be the best place to bring any children under three years old, who cannot understand the concept of respecting the animals' needs.

Age of grandchild: All

Best season: Late spring through early fall

Contact: Henry Vilas Zoo, 702 South Randall Avenue,
Madison, WI 53715 • (608) 266-4733 • www.vilaszoo.org

Also check out:

Milwaukee County Zoo, Milwaukee: www.milwaukeezoo.org

Racine Zoo, Racine: www.racinezoo.org

State Capitol

The capitol is the symbolic center of strength, wisdom and law. It represents a decision made in the early history of the state about location, design and décor that would immediately reflect upon the state and its significance. Wisconsin territory was formed in 1836 with Belmont as the territorial capital. After argument and discussion the leaders of the territory chose Madison to be the capital. But at that time there was no Madison, except on paper. The city which is named after President James Madison grew to become the state capital and the home of the university.

After twenty years, the capitol was found wanting. Too small for a growing bureaucracy, the legislators looked to expand and a new capitol construction project was started. In 1869 the dome was completed, marking the first stage in the construction. In 1882 two wings were added. A fire gutted the capitol in 1904 making a third Madison capitol a necessity. Of course it was bigger. It took until 1915 before all the wings, domes and extras were completed, and it took until 1965 for then-Governor Knowles to hold a dedication ceremony.

Don't be surprised if your grandchildren are in awe as they enter the building. It was designed to give that effect. There is a solemn quality in the marble and the dark trim. The art seems imposing; the dome is high and cathedral-like. Ask your grandchildren how they feel. Does this feel like a special place? Can they sense the power that resides here?

The capitol art, memorials, halls and rooms are filled with a sense of history, but like the laws that are passed each session, the building is a constant work in progress. The changes reflect the times and priorities of the state. In 1937 a large electric "W" was added to the capitol and used extensively during football season. In 1942, World War II brought an end to the waste of energy and the "W" came down.

Perhaps the most surprising fact is that it took until 1968 for the plumbing to be completed. From then on the pipes no longer brought in lake water and for the first time the capitol had safe drinking water. Maybe that is an analogy for the struggle to create the right laws and to do what is needed.

Bonding and bridging:

The lesson you can impart from your own history is that it's the people who make a difference in this country. The building is yours. These are our employees and it is our responsibility to make sure they do a good job, or we vote them out. Is there a more important lesson that we can impart to our grandchildren? Democracy works when individuals demand a voice.

The state capitol is the place to begin. Tell stories, but don't lecture. Share history. Take another walk around the grounds after the tour. Find out who we thought was significant enough to have a statue, visit the war memorials, and see what pictures hang in the halls. Ask your grandchildren what they think is important and help them to draft a letter to their senator or representative. Show them how to participate in government.

A word to the wise:

Make an appointment to visit your senator and representative. Even if you know them at home, they look different in their offices. Get a photo taken with them. Be prepared with a few good questions so the conversation does not lag, but do not make this a lobbying visit. Let your grandchildren feel the importance of government and enjoy the chance to bring a positive taste of politics into their life; they will have enough time later to get frustrated.

Age of grandchild: 10 and up

Best season: Winter (when the legislature is in session)

Contact: Wisconsin State Capitol, 4 East Capitol Square,
Madison, WI 53702 • (608) 266-0382
www.wisconsin.gov/state/capfacts/tour_select.html

Also check out:

Wisconsin government website:
www.wisconsin.gov/state/core/government.html

Wisconsin's first state capitol, Belmont:
www.doj.state.wi.us/kidspage/fun_facts/belmont.htm

My grandfather was a giant of a man . . . When he walked, the earth shook. When he laughed, the birds fell out of the trees. His hair caught fire from the sun. His eyes were patches of sky. ETH CLIFFORD, *THE REMEMBERING BOX*

57

Little Switzerland

If you are looking for snow-capped peaks or sharp outlines of rocky mountains across the skyline you might be disappointed. Certainly there are hills though—nice hills by Wisconsin standards, but not the Alps. However, don't think high, think low. Think of valleys. As in Switzerland, the towns in this region are in the valleys.

This community is known nationwide as "Little Switzerland" and it celebrates its history, its location and its connection to its namesake. Your grandchildren will immediately notice the strange architecture; a look that is very different from other Wisconsin towns. Chalets are the dominant structures, but the

churches, the depot and the street signs all say Switzerland and give the visitor a wonderful sense of place. Today the Swiss make up just one third of the population and they might be outnumbered by people of German descent, but that has not prevented the community from focusing on its Swiss roots.

An economic crisis in Switzerland caused 108 people from Glarus, Switzerland, to come to this southern Wisconsin valley in hopes of carving out new lives. They settled New Glarus in 1845, and subsequent settlers have reached out to keep the connection current.

Take your grandchildren through the historic Swiss village. This is not a reproduction from Switzerland, but buildings erected and businesses started by the Swiss settlers. Fourteen buildings give insight into the daily life, as well as the crafts, like cheese-making that have blossomed throughout Wisconsin. You will find an amazing bee house, a sausage shop, a fire house, a print shop, and a one-room schoolhouse among the buildings you explore.

You can get rooms in the historic New Glarus Hotel or modern Swiss-style lodging if you want to keep the international flavor. Be sure to eat while you are here. Restaurants in town serve Swiss food.

Round out your visit with a bike ride on the Sugar River State Trail and hike in New Glarus Woods State Park in order to experience the beauty that enticed immigrants to put down new roots in this Wisconsin landscape.

Bonding and bridging:

What do you think of when you hear the word "Swiss"? Is it cheese, yodeling, the Matterhorn, banks or neutrality? People, like countries, acquire reputations, good and bad, and once we have a reputation it's hard to change it. Ask your grandchildren if they have an image of Switzerland in their mind and have them describe it. How did they get the image? How do they think people in the rest of the world would describe Wisconsin? Where would they learn or hear about Wisconsin? You might have fun talking about the things that we think are important about the state and what others might think. From this you might be able to talk about our own reputations, what others think about us, as well as what we say and think about others.

A word to the wise:

The Wilhelm Tell Festival on Labor Day and the Heidi Festival in June are real highlights for the entire family, mixing literature, classical music, Swiss legend and lots of creative artistry. Of course the story of Wilhelm Tell explains how he shot an apple off his son's head with an arrow from a crossbow and so helped Switzerland gain its independence. Less frightening than this tale are the live goats, cows and horses that help the actors present the outdoor tale. In mid-June, the story of Heidi is the source of a three-day celebration that combines Swiss heritage, crafts and art, folk dancing, polkas, yodeling, flag throwing and live performances of the Heidi classic.

Age of grandchild: 4 and up

Best season: Summer

Contact: New Glarus Chamber of Commerce, 418 Railroad Street, New Glarus, WI 53574 • (608) 527-2095 • www.swisstown.com

Also check out:

Green County Cheese Days, Monroe: www.cheesedays.com

Swiss Historical Village and Museum, New Glarus: www.swisshistoricalvillage.org

Wilhelm Tell Festival, New Glarus: www.wilhelmtell.org

If you don't know [your family's] history, then you don't know anything. You are a leaf that doesn't know it is part of a tree. MICHAEL CRICHTON

Green County Cheese Days

In a state where people wear foam cheese wedges on their heads to professional football games, how can you let your grandchildren miss out on the world of cheese? Wisconsin is the dairy capital of the world, and if we are going to have pride in our state we should celebrate our prize product. No, not the Packers—the cheese. And to celebrate, there is nothing better than Green County Cheese Days in Monroe.

This event began in 1914 when the local leaders saw that a town in Illinois had a sauerkraut festival. "If they can celebrate sauerkraut, we can do better with a cheese celebration." That is not a direct quote, but close—and in the end they probably did do better. They took the idea, handlettered a sign that read, "FIRST CHEESE DAY COMMITTEE 1914—WE STARTED SOMETHING!" And in nine days it was a fact. So every year there is a September cheese festival.

What will you and your grandchildren do at a cheese festival? You'd better plan on eating. There are many varieties and textures and colors and smells of cheese, and this is a place and time to explore them. Taste them, buy them, have them deep-fried in fat if your heart can stand it.

Take the Green County farm tour to let your grandchildren see where cheese comes from. They might be surprised to see that it does not just appear in the store in plastic wrap, sliced and separated by little pieces of paper.

The highlight of the event is the historic cheesemaking center where guides dressed in Swiss costumes take you on tours of the old, restored depot, a shrine to the history of cheese-making.

Combine Cheese Days with a visit to New Glarus and your grandchildren will be looking for the tickets to Switzerland to continue their experience. But since that is a little expensive, go to the polka lessons with them and get them dizzy instead. Just wait awhile for all the cheese to digest first.

Bonding and bridging:

What foods do we associate with a location? Surely we think of spaghetti and pizza when we say Italy. Some would think of baklava in Greece, tacos in Mexico, sauerkraut in Germany and meatballs in Sweden. What are the foods you and your grandchildren think of? Ask them what food your family should be famous for. What is the food of your town?

Food is important. We have clichés like "food is the way to a man's heart." We devote three times a day, at least, to eating, and spend a lot of our life earning the money to buy food. Talk about the foods you liked when you were your grandchildren's age. How was food different then? Why do we talk about comfort foods? What does that mean and what are they for each of you? This talk might make you hungry, so be ready to pursue one of these comfort foods afterwards.

A word to the wise:

There are two activities that add to your festival experience. First, Green County has at least thirteen factories and outlets where you can buy cheese. Visiting the outlets will make a nice drive through the country and a fun way to taste and choose your cheese delights. Second, the parade is a celebration of both Swiss heritage and cheese-making. Bands, floats and fun in a traditional small town parade make this a wonderful sharing event.

Age of grandchild: 3 and up

Best season: September

Contact: Green County Cheese Days, 1505 Ninth Street,
Monroe, WI 53566 • (608) 325-7771 • www.cheesedays.com

Also check out:

Green County cheese factories:

Decatur Dairy, Brodhead: (608) 897-8661

Edelweiss Town Hall, Monticello: (608) 938-4094

Roth Kase, Monroe: (608) 328-3355

Mineral Point

Communities like Mineral Point date back to the 1820s and 1830s when more than 4,000 men moved into southwestern Wisconsin. They came to mine lead to make pewter, paint, pipes and ammunition. Today we do not hear much about lead mining, but at one time Wisconsin was the world's biggest producer, and the industry was big enough to attract the famous Cornish miners. They settled into limestone homes in a unique area that is preserved as the state historical site called Pendarvis.

Instead of large-scale open pit or deep shaft mining, the early miners dug holes in the hillsides and used some as their homes, while other holes were their mines. These poor conditions gave the miners the nickname "badgers"—a familiar Wisconsin moniker that is now the name for the university's teams.

Mineral Point and its historic site reflect the peak of mining in 1840. By 1844 the miners were leaving for copper, nickel and gold in new places—where the dream of getting rich had not been damaged by hard work and hardship. Mineral Point had a brief flourish of zinc mining, but the real richness of the land was in farming, an industry that would support the region for the next 150 years.

Today the community attracts thousands of visitors who want to experience the unique architecture and history of the region, as well as browse the artisan shops. Your grandchildren will see the architecture and sample the lifestyle of the miners with hikes, visits to historic buildings and the visitor center.

The historic site has kept the limestone houses of the miners well preserved. When you finish seeing the homes, go to the Merry Christmas Mine Hill and walk its trails. This is the mother lode of the region's mining and the reason that all these families stayed here.

Mineral Point was such an important mining town during the boom years that it had a population larger than Milwaukee. But it didn't last. Luckily that history was preserved and Mineral Point became the first city put on the National Register of Historic Sites. Pendarvis Historic Site (formerly Shake Rag Street) remains one of the community highlights.

Bonding and bridging:

Mining serves as a wonderful metaphor for what is permanent and for what is fleeting. We have a history of mining booms—lead, copper, iron ore, silver and gold. Someone is always chasing after a treasure, but what is really valuable?

Ask your grandchildren what is most valuable to them. Of course, they are most valuable to you. And that is the real story. Love, family and home are the things that really give value to life and all the other trinkets and treasure. Talk to them about what is important in life and what they should be cherishing. This is a chance to talk about some very special values.

A word to the wise:

Shake Rag Alley Center for the Arts offers hands-on workshops for people of all ages. If your grandchildren are old enough and have an interest in arts and crafts, you can enroll in a traditional art workshop. You should also go through the visitor center, a wonderful opportunity to do more than just observe the historic lifestyle of the community. It is impossible to go back in time, but activities that allow us to experience the same things our pioneer ancestors did, give us some connection and appreciation.

Age of grandchild: All

Best season: Late spring through fall

Contact: Mineral Point Chamber of Commerce, 225 High Street, Mineral Point, WI 53565 • (608) 987-3201 • www.mineralpoint.com

Also check out:

The Mining Museum, Platteville: www.mining.jamison.museum

Shake Rag Alley Center for the Arts, Mineral Point: www.shakeragalley.com

Grandparents are similar to a piece of string—handy to have around and easily wrapped around the fingers of their grandchildren. Unknown

63

Prairie Villa Rendezvous

The tang of wood smoke, the clang of iron hitting iron, the sight of bearded men in buckskin and the mist rising from the mighty Mississippi will make you and your grandchildren feel that you've been transported back to the mid-1800s, when fur traders came to St. Feriole Island in what would one day become Wisconsin. Here they would rendezvous to socialize and trade their goods with the Fox Indians who had the furs they sought.

The annual Prairie Villa Rendezvous in Prairie du Chien is a reenactment of those long-gone days. Started a little over thirty years ago and sponsored by the Big River Long Rifles and the Prairie du Chien Jaycees, this is the largest rendezvous of its kind in the region. Nearly one hundred reenactors set up camp along the banks of the river and throughout the island. Everything is designed to be as close to the original history as possible.

Just as in days of old when traders, trappers and Native Americans played games of lacrosse, with hundreds of players on each side, so today games are played throughout the weekend by registered and costumed campers. During the rendezvous of old, peace reigned among the rough characters and arms were not used. Today, weapons are allowed for sport. You can watch the women's and children's knife and tomahawk throwing contests and black-powder shooting competition.

More peaceable activities include blacksmithing, weaving, flint knapping, fiddle playing and storytelling. For the older grandchildren, you may want to attend the presentation on 1700s medical practices, just to see how far we've come. When hunger strikes, you can visit the Jaycee's buffalo burger stand or attend the pie auction. The Rendezvous also features a massive flea market, which we could see as a modern-day version of trading.

The Rendezvous is a smorgasbord of sights, sounds and smells that even grandchildren in strollers will find captivating, but it is probably more suitable for grade school-age children. They will be able to recognize that these people are acting parts and representing a time in our history when life was much more simple and difficult. All children love theater and this is living, historic theater.

Bonding and bridging:

Wandering among these colorful characters, with noise and smells accosting you from every angle, is memorable for you and your grandchildren. Don't be surprised if you get a request to come as a participant. Or maybe you would like to suggest that idea to your grandchildren. Either way, you can try to replicate some of the experience closer to home by putting up a tent and camping out for a night, building a campfire and pretending that you are explorers in an earlier time. Even one night in your own yard will give both of you a better sense of living without the luxuries we take for granted, like electricity and running water. What's better than to snuggle down in your sleeping bags, telling stories to one another in the quiet of the night?

A word to the wise:

You don't have to spend your entire visit surrounded by the crowds. There are places to rent boats. Get out on the river and observe the festivities from a different perspective; or find a quiet backwater where you can drift and listen to the birds in the forest, drop a line over the side and see what's biting. The area around Prairie du Chien is also known for the Indian mounds. In fact the original Fort Crawford was built on one such mound, later replaced with the Villa Louis. Just across the river in Harpers Ferry, Iowa, you can visit the Effigy Mounds National Monument, where there are 206 mounds.

Age of grandchild: 3 and up

Best season: Mid-June

Contact: Prairie du Chien Area Chamber of Commerce,
211 South Main, Prairie du Chien, WI 53821
(800) 732-1673 • www.prairieduchien.org/visitors/rendezvous.htm

Also check out:

Cannons and Redcoats, Prairie du Chien (September):
www.fortcrawfordmuseum.com

Great Folle Avoine Fur Trade Rendezvous, Danbury: www.theforts.org

Pike River Rendezvous, Kenosha:
www.kenosha.org/kenevents/events/pike_river_rendezvous.html

Our children grow up so fast. Maybe grandchildren are God's way of giving us a second chance at participating in the miracle of life. UNKNOWN

Villa Louis
Carriage Classic

Everyone loves a parade and almost all children love horses. The Villa Louis Carriage Classic combines the best of both. Set on the grounds of the historic Villa Louis island estate in Prairie du Chien, this horse and carriage event is the largest of its kind in the region. It is appropriate that such an event takes place here because H. Louis Dousman established Artesian Stock Farms onsite in 1884. This country gentleman had stables, paddocks and even a quarter-mile racetrack built to suit his hobby.

True to the era, the entrants in the Carriage Classic dress in Victorian costumes and drive carriages that would be familiar to Mr. Dousman. The September event draws as many as eighty drivers and their stable hands and helpers.

Throughout the weekend, the competitions include cross-country events with artificial and natural hazards, driving competitions that judge the quality of the horse and its training, and reinsmanship—which judges the abilities of the driver to control horse and carriage through an obstacle course. Other contests take the driver out of the carriage and onto the back of the horse to test the versatility and training of both.

Perhaps holding the most appeal for you and your grandchild is the Picnic Class. Contestants drive to a specific location, unharness their horses and set up a picnic, just as people might have done in the late 1800s. Spectators are welcome to walk through and make their own observations and judgments of the costumes, the people and their carriages. It is like walking through time, with the park-like setting a perfect stage for the actors.

Another event not to be missed is called the Concours d'Elegance. In this late-Sunday-afternoon parade, elegant ladies in elaborate hats and long gowns and their formally attired escorts pass by, pulled by their high-stepping steeds. Harnesses jingle and hooves clip-clop in syncopation down the paths.

While many competitions take place inside rings, there are opportunities to talk to the contestants and possibly to pet the horses, but never allow your grandchild to approach a horse without permission from the owner. While these horses are highly trained and used to being in public settings, they are still large and sometimes unpredictable animals.

Bonding and bridging:

Animals in general are a source of mutual interest to grandparents and grandchildren. Horses are one of the more beautiful and have a mystique of power and grace. If you grew up around horses, tell your grandchildren what that was like. If you have chosen to attend this event, chances are good that your grandchildren already love horses.

Talk about the challenges and responsibilities of owning a horse. Do they dream of owning one some day? Let them know that dreams come true only through persistence and patience. I can attest to this fact, since I, too, dreamed of owning a horse all through my childhood. It finally became a reality for me at the age of thirty-seven.

A word to the wise:

Attending an event like this is bound to inspire a wish to ride in a carriage like the ones you've just seen. Luckily this is not a hard to wish to fulfill. All over the state there are businesses that offer horse-drawn rides of one kind or another. (See the list below.) Once you've ridden in a carriage, you may want to branch out and try a hay ride in the fall or a sleigh ride in the winter.

Age of grandchild: 8 and up

Best season: September

Contact: Villa Louis Carriage Classic, PO Box 117, Prairie du Chien, WI 53821 • (608) 326-4436 • www.carriageclassic.com

Also check out:

Mayberry's Carriages, Egg Harbor: www.mayberryscarriages.com

Milwaukee Coach & Carriage, Milwaukee: www.milwaukeecarriage.com

Fantasy Hills Ranch, Delavan: www.fantasyhillsranch.com

My grandkids believe I'm the oldest thing in the world. And after two or three hours with them, I believe it, too. GENE PERRET

Mid-Continent Railway Museum

Do you remember when we were young, when trains were among the most interesting things in the world—the anticipation and excitement of hearing that horn blast in the distance? A train rolling through our neighborhood was a special event. We all gathered and waved, hoping the man in the caboose would wave back. The Mid-Continent Railway Museum has captured some of that magic, allowing us to share it with our grandchildren.

The museum is located just outside North Freedom, a small town with a wonderful name, but hardly one we have had on our travel itinerary. It is south of Wisconsin Dells and north of Madison; west of Baraboo and east of Reedsburg. It is a perfect place with no distractions, which allows its visitors to concentrate on the rural depot, the tracks and the trains.

Arriving at the depot you are immediately impressed by the multiple tracks and the variety of engines and cars on them. These are working cars, trains that have been given loving attention and now shine in the sun for you to inspect as though they were in their prime. Surrounded by vintage buildings, they have been moved to the site so we see the trains in their historic role (1895–1915).

If your grandchildren are enjoying the Thomas the Train popularity, they will also recognize the water tower, crossing shed and all the signals. There is a coach shed, engine house and car shop on one side of the road with the depot and display shed on the other. In the open buildings you can walk around and sometimes go into some of the inventory that includes thirteen steam locomotives, thirty-eight passenger cars, thirty-one freight cars, twenty-one cabooses and fifteen pieces of service equipment. There is a lot of railroad history here and because of Thomas your grandchildren will be more familiar with the terms and cars than you might expect.

But the real experience is the fifty-minute train ride on tracks laid down by the museum volunteers on seven miles of a former branch line of the Chicago and North Western Railway that runs through the scenic Baraboo Hills. The sound of the wheels on the track, the steam, the whistle and the movement that is only found on railroads makes the day and the memories.

Bonding and bridging:

It's hard for children to realize how important the railroad was in opening the West and in the commerce of Wisconsin. Towns survived if the railroad came through and collapsed if it didn't. This presents an opportunity for you to discuss actions and consequences.

There are some consequences for most things that a grandchild or grandparent does—the grade we get depends upon the homework we did or did not do. How we treat others influences how they will treat us in the future. Just like our communities, we are influenced by our choices and the choices of others. Discuss how decisions affect our lives, our family, our school and our town. Discuss how each of us must think about many things when we make choices.

A word to the wise:

The drive to and from experiences like this can either be long and boring or can add to the experience. Try to look at the variety of vehicles you see on the road, on the farms and along your route. What roles have vehicles played in our history? And don't forget to observe the horses, cattle and dogs. Both horses and oxen pulled carts, and dogs pulled the travois. Our species has a history of transportation all the way back to the beginning of civilization.

Age of grandchild: All

Best season: Late spring through early fall

Contact: Mid-Continent Railway Museum, E8948 Diamond Hill Road, North Freedom, WI 53951 • (608) 522-4261 • www.midcontinent.org

Also check out:

East Troy Electric Railroad Museum, East Troy: www.easttroyrr.org

Fennimore Railroad Historical Society Museum, Fennimore: www.fennimore.com/railmuseum

National Railroad Museum, Green Bay: www.nationalrrmuseum.org

Riverside & Great Northern Railway, Wisconsin Dells: www.randgn.com

Few things are more delightful than grandchildren fighting over your lap. Doug Larson

International Crane Foundation

Twenty-one years ago we were married on an April morning. At the close of the ceremony we saw a pair of sandhilll cranes flying overhead. They circled twice, calling the whole time and then flew onward. We looked at one another and smiled broadly, knowing that in Asian cultures cranes are symbols of longevity and fidelity. Taking our grandchildren to the International Crane Foundation (ICF) was a fitting and fun excursion. It can be for you, too—even if cranes don't fit into your personal family history.

Cranes are the most endangered family of birds in the world, and the ICF is the only place where you can see all fifteen species. There are over a hundred cranes living at the facility, but most are not on exhibit because breeding

cranes are very sensitive to disturbance. The birds are elegant and stately in appearance. If you're lucky, you might get to see and hear a pair perform a duet dance, something they do in courtship or when they are defending their territory.

After leaving the visitor center you can wander on the paved path (approximately half a mile) to the Johnson Exhibit Pod, a series of enclosures in a wheel formation where you can see the various crane species. You can choose to do a self-guided tour with tape recorders (available at the gift shop), or you can take a guided tour which usually lasts one-and-a-half to two hours. You should also be aware that there isn't a lot of shade along the pathway, so be sure to wear a hat and have sunscreen along. There are benches throughout the site, too.

Covering 225 acres, the ICF has a variety of nature trails you can wander (totaling a little over two miles). They will take you through restored prairie, wetlands and oak savanna—all habitats that cranes depend upon in the wild.

Families can pick up a free packet of activities at the gift shop to incorporate into their visit. These include scavenger hunts, bird watching basics, nature journaling and more.

The ICF is a unique setting for a morning or afternoon visit. Begin or end the trip with a picnic lunch at the site. Both picnic grounds and a picnic shelter are available.

Bonding and bridging:

Be sure to visit the Amoco Whooping Crane Exhibit. This covered amphitheatre has benches facing an exhibit with a naturally landscaped pond and a pair of whooping cranes, the world's most endangered crane. You can sit and relax in the shade and just enjoy the scenery, talking about all of the birds you've seen. If it's spring or summer, you may see their chicks, too.

This is a good place to talk about how important it is for us to preserve habitat for wildlife. Ask your grandchild why it's important to preserve a variety of animals in the world. They may not have an answer, but you can help them to think about the importance of diversity. There are displays in the exhibit that help explain this critical topic.

A word to the wise:

If your grandchildren are old enough, consider participating in the Annual Midwest Crane Count held in April of each year. Begun in 1976, it is one of the largest citizen-based inventories in the world. This is what is known as "citizen science," and it will give your grandchildren a chance to contribute important information about the abundance and distribution of cranes in the Upper Midwest. In the 1930s, an estimated twenty-five pairs of sandhill cranes resided in Wisconsin. In 2000, the count tallied more than 13,000 sandhill cranes. For helping to collect valuable crane data, you will receive results later in the year, with a certificate for free admission to the ICF. To learn more, contact the ICF or go to their website.

Age of grandchild: 3 and up

Best season: Spring (and summer)

Contact: International Crane Foundation, E11376 Shady Lane Road, Baraboo, WI 53913 • (608) 356-9462 • www.savingcranes.org

Also check out:

Henry Vilas Zoo, Madison: www.vilaszoo.org

Milwaukee County Zoo, Milwaukee: www.milwaukeezoo.org

Racine Zoo, Racine: www.racinezoo.org

Circus World Museum

The circus is coming! Not too long ago, that was a sound that got every child excited. The circus was a blizzard of movement, color and lights, exotic people and animals, and exciting new possibilities beneath canvas. It was the ultimate in entertainment, before entertainment became a projected image and an electronic experience.

The circus dates back to the Romans and was a little over the top—chariot races, lions and contests that ended in death. Fortunately, tradition shifted from the uglier components of the Roman Circus and focused on traveling troupes of acrobats and performers in the Dark Ages. After the War of 1812 the rolling circus came into vogue in America. In 1884, five brothers in Baraboo, Wisconsin—Alfred, Albert, Otto, Charles and John Ringling—began their own, homemade performances and rose in fame and fortune, purchasing the rest of the circuses that rode the rails or marched into town with a big top. Eventually, they became the Ringling Brothers and Barnum and Bailey Circus—literally the "greatest show on Earth."

Circus World Museum captures much of the magic as it brings together rides, parade wagons, animals, international acrobats, clowns of all descriptions, music and sweets in a sprawling complex of hands-on learning and nostalgia. There are exhibits, circus acts, circus wagons and other memorabilia. Be ready for color, costume, animals, rides and all the energy of the circus that we grandparents experienced. There are foods to eat, acts to attend and hands-on experiences to add to the grandchildren's day.

But remember that they do not have our connection with circuses. Circuses still travel to large cities, but their shows are in auditoriums; the distance from the acts, the loss of the smells of the animals mixing with the scent of popcorn and cotton candy changes the experience. Today it is a spectacle; back then it was an experience. So the grandparent can guide the children through this nostalgic trip.

What you see as a grandparent is not the same thing that the children see. You can bridge the gap in generations. If your grandchildren are young, they are not as jaded by the electronic games, so this can be as awesome for them as it was for you.

Bonding and bridging:

There are some things that we as grandparents remember from our childhood that we can share with our grandchildren. I remember the circus coming to Rice Lake, Wisconsin; the parade down Main Street and the bustle at the fairgrounds as workers set up the big top. We were wide-eyed in hopes of seeing one of the "freaks" and amazed by the elephants doing all the heavy lifting. If you have similar memories, it doesn't seem that long ago when we sat in the wooden bleachers and watched the performers in their outlandish costumes, does it?

Can you explain how we waited for the clowns and got nervous when we heard the roars of the lions when the tamer entered the cage? The circus stopped work in the fields, closed stores and brought everyone together. What compares to that today?

A word to the wise:

Ride the elephant or the camel. It is not much of a ride, but just the thought of being on the back of these traditional circus animals is enough. Our grandson, Matthew, loved it and felt a connection with the animal afterward. Don't just pay and leave. Watch the animals, talk to them and treat them with respect as circus performers. This kind of ethical experience will help your grandchildren understand that we have unusual relationships with animals on the farm, circus or zoo. For our future, we need to respect and understand all life forms. This is a good place to start.

Age of grandchild: 3 and up

Best season: Mid-May through early September

Contact: Circus World Museum, 550 Water Street, Baraboo, WI 53913
(608) 356-8341 • www.wisconsinhistory.org/circusworld

Also check out:

International Clown Hall of Fame, West Allis: www.theclownmuseum.org

Bringing up a family should be an adventure, not an anxious discipline in which everybody is constantly graded for performance. MILTON R. SAPERSTEIN

Dells Duck Ride

The Wisconsin Dells has always been a landscape of excess, an amusement park disguised as a city. But behind the facades, the colors, the water slides, the motorized vehicles, the random themes and the massive temptations to spend money, there is a beautiful river that gives the community its name.

Early maps designated this The Dalles of the Wisconsin River, a name repeated in The Dalles of the Eau Claire River and St. Croix Dalles, which became Dells. Early travelers used the word "dalles" to describe a river moving between cliffs in a narrow channel. French explorers and voyageurs used this term to define similar places which might impact their river travel. As early as 1856, the *Wisconsin Mirror* editor wrote that the "wild, romantic scenery of the dells will always make them a place for resort seekers of pleasure," predicting its present tourism draw.

Ninety years later came the Ducks. Built by General Motors, the Ducks were constructed for storming the beach at Normandy and other amphibious assaults from 1942 to 1944. Over 2,000 landed at Normandy and thousands more stormed the beaches on the Pacific front.

In 1946, right after World War II, Mel Flath brought surplus army amphibians to Lake Delton and began to give tourists rides on water and land. This unusual ride preceded Tommy Bartlett's water ski show by a few years and established the pattern for what is recognized as the Wisconsin Dells today.

Most rides spin too much, go too fast or are too contrived for my tastes (and maybe yours), so get on board a Duck and sit next to your grandchildren, laugh and explore together.

Your grandchildren will not know what amphibious assault vehicles are. They will not know World War II history, so they will not know what to expect. Don't tell them. Let them enjoy the surprises as the vehicle drives through the forest and fern glens, then plunges into the river. You will float the river, pass by sandstone cliffs and river forests, then climb up into a creek, back into a lake and finally end on a path through the forests.

Bonding and bridging:

For the most part we think commercial operations do enough promoting and we are not looking for ways for grandparents to spend money, but this location is unique in its historical and natural features. Along with Tommy Bartlett's water ski show, this is the original historic Dells experience. It is a good context to talk about what's fun.

What do your grandchildren think is fun? Listen to them and compare their ideas with what you did when you were their age. Tell them about your games, toys and experiences. Do your activities sound fun to them? If so, can you try some together? Why is it different today? Who influences what we think is fun? How do we make good choices?

A word to the wise:

These amphibians are the surplus fleet of the vehicles of war that meant both life and death for our military. They formed the fleet in 1946 but were never put into service. However, they are still part of the military story. Riding these 1940s vehicles is a connection with our own history, another story to enrich the shared generational ride.

Age of grandchild: 2 and up

Best season: Summer

Contact:

Dells Glacial Park Tours (Dells Army Ducks),
1550 Wisconsin Dells Parkway, Wisconsin Dells, WI 53965
(608) 254-6080 • www.dellsducks.com

Original Wisconsin Ducks, 1890 Wisconsin Dells Parkway,
PO Box 117, Wisconsin Dells, WI 53965
(608) 254-8751 • www.wisconsinducktours.com

Also check out:

Apostle Islands Cruise Service, Bayfield: www.apostleisland.com

Betty Lou Cruises, Madison: www.bettyloucruises.com

Dells Boat Tours, Wisconsin Dells: www.dellsboats.com

Door County Cruises, Sturgeon Bay: www.doorcountycruises.com

The closest friends I have made all through life have been people who also grew up close to a loved and living grandmother or grandfather. Margaret Mead

Water Parks at the Wisconsin Dells

A plastic tube with water running through it is your invitation to the newest roller coaster-style experience. Climb the stairs in your bathing suit. Look into the maze of tubes and commit yourself to a wild ride. The taller the slide, the more energy you will achieve and the faster you will go! Whether you ride on a mat or just your own body, the water provides the lubrication to send you on a wild careening adventure. The variety of slides is amazing in the Dells, which have found a way to be a year-round adventure and vacation site.

The Dells have the highest concentration of indoor waterparks in the world! At this writing the African themed Kalahari Resort has the distinction of being the world's largest indoor waterpark. The superlatives just keep on going. There are uphill roller coasters, tube rides, the longest lazy river ride in the U.S. (of course) and the FlowRider with a flow of 50,000 gallons per minute. The Great Wolf Lodge, another Dells waterpark, has a fifty-three foot vertical drop!

Then you add the curves. The distance to the bottom is measured not just in vertical distance. The slides snake around, whipping you in all directions. You are being pulled down not only by gravity, but you are working against gravity in each curve—with your body wanting to go straight and the tube making you go against your own inertia. Fortunately they know that the curves must actually go up at these turns or you would be launched at the first turn.

For 150 years this area has been the playground of Wisconsin with Ducks, boats and outdoor amusement parks. The owners began in the 1980s to replace the indoor pool with plastic designed to send swimming-suit-clad customers on a whirlwind, wet ride. Then in late 1994, the Polynesian Resort Hotel changed the recreation world when it opened the area's first indoor water play area.

Their intention was to entice customers in June, the slow month. They began a "gold rush" that was followed by numerous resorts and changed the Dells' face and season. Some of these rides may be too much for grandparents and grandchildren, but luckily there are all levels and you can choose the ones you want to experience and those you only want to watch.

Bonding and bridging:

If you are able to do some of the slides—even the minor ones—it will be a shock to your grand-children or the children around. Too often grand-parents are described as "old" in a way that indi-cates we are incapable of playing or doing other physical things.

Sometimes that's true, but often grandparents are underestimated, and it is good for your grandchildren to see you play. They learn that playing is a good thing, not just for children. You can open up a much more enjoyable life for them by exposing them to this fact. "Grow up!" is a terrible thing to tell anyone. Grow wiser and grow healthier, but the implication of those two words implies that having fun is only for young children.

A word to the wise:

Want to stay dry for a little while and have a real contrasting experience? Visit one of the state's historic sites and one of the true attractions of Wisconsin Dells: H. H. Bennett's photo studio. This site combines a variety of features—the history of photography, one of the rare remnants of the old Wisconsin Dells business community and a photographic history of the region before today's flood of entertainments. Mr. Bennett returned from the Civil War with an injury that prevented him from pursuing his career as a carpenter. So instead he turned to the camera and the beauty of the Wisconsin Dells. He said, "It is easier to pose nature and less trouble to please." His claim to fame was his stereoscopic views of the dells. Grandparents might remember their own experience with the View-Master, an outgrowth of this format.

Age of grandchild: 3 and up

Best season: All

Contact: Wisconsin Dells Visitor and Convention Bureau,
701 Superior Street, Wisconsin Dells, WI 53965
(800) 223-3557 • www.wisdells.com

Also check out:

Lodge at Cedar Creek, Wausau: www.lodgeatcedarcreek.com

Tundra Lodge Resort & Waterpark, Green Bay: www.tundralodge.com

Family faces are magic mirrors. Looking at people who belong to us, we see the past, present and future. Gail Lumet Buckley

Monroe County Biking

This is more than just a trail ride. Monroe County has trails, country roads, spectacular scenery, small communities and Amish farms. Best known for the Elroy-Sparta State Trail there are many more options that can make a day, a weekend or a week of pedaling pleasure. Depending on time, age of grandchildren and your conditioning, you can choose multiple options, but choose at least one. Sparta calls itself the Bicycling Center of the World and boasts a thirty-foot statue of Ben Biken on an old-time high-wheeler bicycle, and it's a good place to start a two-wheel exploration.

There are 101 miles of bicycle trails here with the Elroy-Sparta trail running one direction and the LaCrosse River State Trail going the other. In addition, this is a great county of country road pedaling—something that should be reserved for older grandchildren. Choose the option that suits the family. It is not how many miles you cover but how much fun you have and how much you learn that counts.

The Elroy-Sparta trail is thirty-two miles long on the abandoned Chicago and North Western Railroad bed and passes through three rock tunnels. The Kendall and Wilton tunnels are one-quarter mile long and the Norwalk tunnel is three-quarters of a mile long. There is a fee for riding on the trail—something we should be pleased to pay to keep it in great shape for our two-wheelers. This is the first Rails to Trails bike trail in the country. Another bike trail has been added to the southern end—the 400 trail, which adds the scenic valley of the Baraboo River to this complex of 101 miles and four trails.

The La Crosse River State Trail is 21.5 miles and connects the Elroy-Sparta State Trail with the Great River State Trail. It travels past farms, prairie remnants, woods and trout streams in the landscape known as Coulee Country.

Finally there is the option to bike the country roads through Coulee Country. (The name is from the French meaning flowing.) But what you get is a rolling landscape of hills and vistas, forests and streams. It is Amish country, dotted with farms and small towns. A bike ride in this country is a sampler of cows, sheep, goats and horses. In the towns are bakeries and cheese factories that make great spots for snack breaks. The Amish wagons, lifestyles and fashion are intriguing and add to the country adventure.

Bonding and bridging:

Going slow is disappearing in our lifestyles. We want faster planes, trains and automobiles. Gravel roads become blacktop roads, and blacktop roads get wider and wider until they become freeways. So here you are in Coulee Country— Monroe County. The Amish who live here still travel by horse-drawn wagon and walk or bicycle.

Getting on the bicycle is not only healthy, it is also a chance to see details, to talk while you pedal, to stop and see the cows or smell the flowers. It is a chance to talk about slowing down. Your grandchildren will want to speed down hills—let them, but don't let that distract you from the sense of leisure a day like this can provide. Ask them how much they have seen and compare that with the details that they saw on the drive to this area.

A word to the wise:

Bring water and energy food, and take breaks. Nothing detracts from a biking experience like exhaustion, dehydration or hunger. Small towns provide food and drinks, but have water and some good snacks like trail mix, dehydrated fruits or energy bars. Avoiding headaches and muscle cramps of dehydration is easy if you keep a routine of a swallow of water every half hour of exercise.

Age of grandchild: 8 and up

Best season: Late spring through early fall

Contact: Elroy-Sparta State Trail Headquarters, PO Box 297, Kendall, WI 54638 • (608) 463-7109 • www.elroy-sparta-trail.com

Also check out:

400 State Trail: www.400statetrail.org

Great River State Trail: www.dnr.state.wi.us/org/land/parks/specific/greatriver

Glacial Drumlin State Trail: www.glacialdrumlin.com

La Crosse River State Trail: www.lacrosseriverstatetrail.org

Madison area biking trails: www.ci.madison.wi.us/transp/bicycle.html

The charm of a woodland road lies not only in its beauty but in anticipation. Around each bend may be a discovery, an adventure. DALE REX COMAN

Warrens Cranberry Festival

Thanksgiving is a legendary day of feasting which we still enjoy, with two of the most indigenous foods in America—turkey and cranberries. Many people know that Ben Franklin wanted to name the wild turkey our national bird, instead of the eagle. (Not one of his better ideas.) Can you imagine eating our national symbol? Today we eat domesticated versions of those originals.

Truly wild cranberries, like most other wild berries, are tiny and difficult to harvest, but over the years, growers have developed the large cranberry we serve at our Thanksgiving dinners today. It grows in the bogs of the North

Country and produces a tart flavor unlike any other fruit. It is harvested in the autumn and then paired with our favorite traditional poultry. The cranberry is the Wisconsin State Fruit.

The Wisconsin Cranberry Discovery Center was created in Warrens to help families learn the significance of this natural product. The community and center host the Cranberry Festival in late September. You might think that such a festival would be low-key, but be prepared. With three miles of booths and vendors and 100,000 visitors, this is a major event. It's like a farmers market, as well as a celebration, and special meals, arts and crafts will provide a background for you and your grandchildren as you wander around the unique landscape of the cranberry marsh (bog).

Growing cranberries creates a habitat that looks very natural. There are birds to observe and native plants to discover. The famous Wisconsin naturalist, Aldo Leopold, credited the cranberry bogs with saving the sandhill cranes, and you might be lucky enough to see one while you play and roam.

The parade is a fun event in cranberry colors, and the tour of the cranberry marsh where harvesters have raised the water level around the tiny cranberry vines is a real pleasure. This floats the berries to the top, where they make a colorful pattern in the water. The berries will actually be harvested in early October. (Glacial Lake Cranberries offers tours throughout harvest season.)

After an event like this you'll be ready for Thanksgiving. This will make the meal more significant for your grandchildren—just show them the turkey.

Bonding and bridging:

Take a seat in the Discovery Center's old ice cream parlor and sample the combination of cranberries with ice cream. Nothing beats ice cream for crossing generational lines, and this setting is perfect. The parlor is not a re-creation of an old soda fountain; it is the real thing. Steele's Drug Store in Tomah used this counter and stool combination from the 1930s until 1973, and it has been given loving care to make it feel like new.

Grandparents can relate to the setting, but it is new for grandchildren and you can talk about the flavors, candies and treats you loved as a child. Ask them about their favorite candies, ice creams and flavors. My grandfather always had a box of Fanny Farmer chocolates in his desk drawer, and I still think of him whenever offered a piece of box candy.

A word to the wise:

The Wisconsin Cranberry Discovery Center near Warrens is the place to finish your tour of Cranberry Country. This old cranberry warehouse has historical displays that range from dugout canoes to the modern cranberry paddles and traditional crafts for harvesting. In addition, you can have cranberry ice cream cones in the Ice Cream Parlor, taste cranberry pie in the test kitchen, and try other treats from the bakery. It's good to leave with a tart taste in your mouth.

Age of grandchild: 8 and up

Best season: Fall

Contact: Warrens Cranberry Festival, 402 Pine Street, Warrens, WI 54666 • (608) 378-4200 • www.cranfest.com

Also check out:

Glacial Lake Cranberries, Wisconsin Rapids:
www.cranberrylink.com/glacial.html

Stone Lake Cranberry Festival, Stone Lake (October):
www.stonelakecranberryfestival.com

Wisconsin Cranberry Discovery Center, Warrens:
www.discovercranberries.com

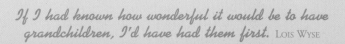

If I had known how wonderful it would be to have grandchildren, I'd have had them first. Lois Wyse

St. Croix National Scenic Riverway

In 1968 America recognized its river heritage and designated a group of rivers that were pristine, accessible and represented our heritage. The St. Croix-Namekagon river system was one of the first of eight river systems to get this national status, and it still deserves our attention and our visits. These two rivers are beautiful streams that provide us with 252 miles of great fishing, bird watching, canoeing, camping, hiking, visitor centers and sightseeing.

Choose a place near you to get introduced to the St. Croix River. The great thing about rivers is their constant changes. Each bend in the river presents a

new view; each overlook has a different vista. The current changes, the birds vary, the plants shift with the soils and sun exposure. Interstate State Park is a dramatic canyon with cliffs of ancient volcanic rocks, and Governor Knowles State Forest has beautiful trails to explore.

The primary visitor center is at St. Croix Falls and has books, a slide show and exhibits. If you have checked it out, read about it and talked about it, it's time to get on the water and a canoe is the best craft for exploring its wildness.

Choosing a canoe route has many factors. What is the water level? What is your experience level? How old are your grandchildren? Have you given your grandchildren canoe lessons? How much time do you have? How will you do the shuttle? Unless you choose to canoe on one of the reservoirs you will be going downstream and that means that you need a way to get back to your car. Outfitters on the river can take care of all of the logistics.

A canoe is quiet, so you can talk or listen to the bird calls. You can quietly float close to beavers and muskrats, mergansers and wood ducks. My life changed the first time I got in a canoe. Each corner opened up a new wonder and connected me with the natural world.

Bring food and snacks, a fishing pole, a day pack, a camera and binoculars. Set out to discover what can be seen and you will not be disappointed.

Bonding and bridging:

The ability to both listen quietly and talk makes canoeing a shared capsule of learning. Drifting is a great chance to talk about the world, life and priorities. It removes the outside influences that can come between you and your grandchildren. Here the craft is your connection to one another, to the river and to history.

Cast your lure in the water, sit on the canoe bottom and drift with the current, listen, observe and reflect. How many places in the world allow you to have that kind of experience with your grandchildren?

A word to the wise:

Canoeing looks easier than it is. The boat is not designed to just move in a straight line; it must be steered. It is not the bow paddler's fault when it goes side to side; it is a failure of the team. Take time to learn on a lake. Take some lessons. Most important is the practice you get and the knowledge of the strokes you need. When you are arguing about why the canoe isn't going straight, you are not bonding. Sliding under branches, hitting rocks and tipping over do not make for quality sharing time. Put the work into making it a good experience. Preparation is the key.

Age of grandchild: 9 and up

Best season: Spring through fall

Contact: St. Croix National Scenic Riverway, 401 North Hamilton Street, St. Croix Falls, WI 54024 • (715) 483-2274 • www.nps.gov/sacn

Also check out:

Brule River State Forest, Brule: (715) 372-5678
www.dnr.wi.gov/org/land/forestry/StateForests/SF-Brule

Buckhorn State Park, Necedah: (608) 565-2789
www.dnr.wi.gov/org/land/parks/specific/buckhorn

Governor Knowles State Forest, Grantsburg: (715) 463-2898
www.dnr.wi.gov/org/land/forestry/stateforests/SF-Knowles

Interstate State Park, St. Croix Falls: (715) 483-3747
www.dnr.state.wi.us/org/land/parks/specific/interstate

Forts Folle Avoine Historical Park

Step back to a time when the French-Canadian Voyageurs traveled on foot and in canoes, when the beaver was their quarry, and the Ojibwe and Dakota did not live on reservations. At Forts Folle Avoine Historical Park you are in Wisconsin between 1600 and 1850, and you are about to explore the fort and Indian village on the banks of the Yellow River in Burnett County.

First discovered in 1969, a full scale archaeological exploration provided the basis for the re-creation of this Indian village and fort. Your grandchildren and

you will walk a path that takes you back in time, and costumed guides will help you make the transition to the period.

This site is very exciting for history buffs because both the XY and North West companies built structures next to the Ojibwe encampment, but for you and your grandchildren, it is exciting to see the contrast in styles and buildings. The Ojibwe used birchbark and the voyageurs built with logs.

The real treat is the interpretations from the costumed guides. You can learn about the crafts that helped them in their day-to-day living, the food and resources of the forests, the ways they handled the insects, built their homes, stayed dry in the rain and warm in the cold. This is a living history experience, and it is good to ask questions of the guides and explore the ideas about this forest life.

Your grandchildren will enjoy the costumes of the voyageurs and the Indians. It is like a movie set to them, but it is based on reality, and the information you get here connects to the land, to history and to the convergence of streams that enter the St. Croix, the Mississippi and the Great Lakes. This was early commerce, an international trade based on the value of a beaver skin.

When you are done, you can spend some time wandering the trails that criss-cross the eighty acres of land.

Bonding and bridging:

History is often about memorizing dry and distant dates and battles, a dry and distant learning experience—but not here. At historic sites we want to encourage grandchildren to ask questions, to explore and—where allowed—to touch and experience history.

We want to encourage their curiosity and invite them to explore new ideas, so try to combine reading, writing and drawing with visiting the sites. Discuss with the children what they saw. Did they understand what these people were saying? Can they understand that this is about events and culture from a hundred years ago? Do not assume that they make the connection. It is one thing to see people in a play; it is another thing to see that the play is based on another reality.

A word to the wise:

If you want your grandchildren to have the most exciting and involved experience in history, come to the July Rendezvous. This is an encampment of historical reenactors, people who enjoy dressing up and participating in an era they find inspiring. They usually have crafts for sale, and their children sleep with them in their tents and dress to the period. Seeing other children in costume really inspires your grandchildren. The reenactors cook over fires, dress with great authenticity and are very happy to share their knowledge and enthusiasm. But beware. Hang around these people, and you'll be reserving a place for your family to camp at the next Rendezvous!

Age of grandchild: 5 and up

Best season: Summer

Contact: Forts Folle Avoine Historical Park, 8500 County Road U, Danbury, WI 54830 • (715) 866-8890 • www.theforts.org

Also check out:

Fort Howard, Heritage Hill State Park (Green Bay): www.heritagehillgb.org

Fort LaPointe, LaPointe (Madeline Island): www.madelineisland.com/history.htm

A child needs a grandparent, anybody's grandparent, to grow a little more securely into an unfamiliar world. CHARLES AND ANN MORSE

Lumberjack World Championships

In 1850, my great-great grandfather left Liechtenstein, crossed the ocean from Europe to New Orleans, then moved up the Mississippi looking for work, land and a future. Knapp Stout and Company gave him a commission as a timber cruiser and sent him to the Upper Chippewa River Valley to seek the company's fortune. The beaver were already trapped, and gold was not to be found, but the treasure of Wisconsin was right in front of him and everyone else who immigrated to Wisconsin. It was the forest.

Today you can show your grandchildren the northern forest and celebrate the exciting life of the lumberjack—one of the truly colorful characters of America. He was the wool-shirted counterpart to the French-Canadian voyageur and the western mountain man. Lumberjacks' lives were anything but easy. They were strong, determined outdoorsmen who depended on skills that demanded strength and coordination, as well as ability to accept danger as a constant companion. To celebrate these skilled men of the forest, the Lumberjack World Championships were created in Hayward in 1969.

This colorful competition has fast action. Your grandchildren will see men almost run up bare poles, roll logs in the pond and compete in tests of their stamina, as well as their skill. Competitors come from all over the U.S. and beyond, to challenge themselves in events like the Springboard Chopping, ninety-foot open climb, ax throw, boom run and the men's and women's log rolling competitions. There are over twenty-one events, with more than one hundred competitors, men and women.

The arena will captivate your grandchildren. Sitting on bleachers on two sides of an old logging pond puts you close to the action and the splashes. Over 12,000 people attend throughout the weekend, so it's wise to come early to get a good seat. A little food and beverage, a hike between events, and you are ready for a great time.

All events are scheduled for specific performance times each day. Competitors who have the best times on Friday advance to Saturday's show, and Saturday's winners advance to the finals on Sunday.

Bonding and bridging:

Very few of us can say we worked as lumberjacks, but most adults—especially grandfathers—have at some point in our lives held an ax and chopped wood. Maybe it was only a hatchet in Boy Scouts, but there is a connection to the past.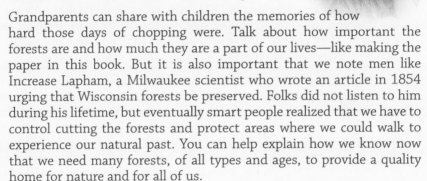

Grandparents can share with children the memories of how hard those days of chopping were. Talk about how important the forests are and how much they are a part of our lives—like making the paper in this book. But it is also important that we note men like Increase Lapham, a Milwaukee scientist who wrote an article in 1854 urging that Wisconsin forests be preserved. Folks did not listen to him during his lifetime, but eventually smart people realized that we have to control cutting the forests and protect areas where we could walk to experience our natural past. You can help explain how we know now that we need many forests, of all types and ages, to provide a quality home for nature and for all of us.

A word to the wise:

Our son-in-law participated in these shows when he was a teenager, and he suggests that the best to see is the chopping or the power saw (souped up chainsaws). We also recommend staying to see the Dock Dog World Championships, held at intermission each day. In these events, dogs run and leap off a dock in an attempt to grab a padded dummy suspended over the water. Their enthusiasm and athleticism is worth the price of admission. Almost everyone can relate to the sheer exuberance of a yellow or black lab.

Age of grandchild: 5 and up

Best season: Summer

Contact: Lumberjack World Championships,
PO Box 666, Hayward, WI 54843
(715) 634-2484 • www.lumberjackworldchampionships.com

Also check out:

Klondike Days, Eagle River: www.klondikedays.org

National Fresh Water Fishing Hall of Fame and Museum

Try to imagine being the bait. Imagine a big musky, a really big musky ready to pounce. The mouth opens and suddenly you are inside. Wow—what an image. Was that what the designer thought when the National Fresh Water Fishing Hall of Fame was designed? This is not a building but rather a big musky that you enter, and from there on you are ready to explore the world of fishing and the gadgets, designs and tools that have become part of the legends and history of game fishing.

Four stories high, this is the king of fish, and inside you can look at vintage lures, antique rods and reels, outboard motors and more angling paraphernalia. Maybe you will find some that are in your tackle box. Maybe you will find some that are so strange you wonder how it ever got inside anyone's tackle box. Anglers are like all enthusiasts—when they get hooked they are ready to buy anything. The lure of more equipment is perhaps a stronger attraction to the angler than the lure of the fish.

The big musky is the eye catcher, but there are four more buildings that make up the main museum and house the theater and the displays. Climbing to the top means going out the mouth of the giant fish and getting a look at the Hayward lakes area. There are additional large fish, like the bluegill, rainbow trout, smallmouth bass, perch and the coho salmon, all part of the site's sea of fishes and fun for grandchildren. Your family might be so inspired after your visit that you head to a nearby lake and drop a line in the water.

The museum was the idea of Bob Kutz of Hayward in 1960, but he and his wife struggled to find support until the Jim Beam Company came through with a ten-year distribution of fish decanters that gave the Hall of Fame some financial backing. The institute grew in both size and stature and added their own catch-and-release program, a wonderful way to promote conservation, while giving credit to the records of those who release their catches.

This museum is a testament to the allure of lures, the beauty of fish, the variations of angling, and the history of the sport. But we are pleased to say that it is also a place that teaches the conservation of resources and an ethic that will promote fishing forever.

Bonding and bridging:

We know children model the behaviors they have seen in adults. How often do we think about the impact of our pleasures and our responsibilities to protect the natural world? Or the way our actions look to our grandchildren?

The museum helps you find some important lessons that you can share while enjoying both the museum and the sport of fishing. They suggest the following ethical behaviors for you to do and to talk about with your grandchildren:

- Get rid of lead. The sinkers that end up on the bottom of the lake poison the fish, the loons and anything else that eats them.

- Go to a four-cycle engine instead of a two-stroke. They are cleaner and are quieter, too.

- Take a trash bag in your tackle box and clean up your fishing site.

A word to the wise:

The Hall of Fame features legendary anglers, guides and scribes who entertained and informed us by their writings in newspapers, magazines and books. In every endeavor we have the potential to be special. We decide how we pursue our sports, our careers and our ethics. Halls of Fame are wonderful recognition for special people, but more, they are inspirations for us when we remove self-imposed limitations and believe in ourselves.

Age of grandchild: 4 and up

Best season: April through October

Contact: National Fresh Water Fishing Hall of Fame and Museum, 10360 Hall of Fame Drive, Hayward, WI 54843 (715) 634-4440 • www.freshwater-fishing.org

Also check out:

Madison Fishing Expo, Madison: (608) 245-1040 • www.madfishexpo.com

Sheldon's, Inc., Antigo: (715) 623-2382 • www.mepps.com

I don't intentionally spoil my grandkids. It's just that correcting them often takes more energy than I have left. GENE PERRET

89

Old Firehouse and Police Museum

There's something special about a person in uniform, and children are fascinated by the costumes of police, firefighters, soldiers, marching band members and all others we encounter in their special uniforms. But firefighters and police officers are heroes in our everyday lives. We teach our children to trust them, seek them out, respect and admire them.

In Superior, the Old Firehouse and Police Museum offers a glimpse at the lives of heroes of the past. Old Station No. 4 is fascinating for its 1898-style that combines the bold brick edifice of a prospering frontier city with the

"castle-like" corner. You can picture the firemen sitting outside, a Dalmatian nearby, maybe a checkers game and the gleaming fire wagons waiting to be pulled by horse or humans.

A lot has changed since the days when this was a new structure, but not the danger of fire and the need for brave people to fight the flames. It is the last of Superior's old-style firehouses and was slated for destruction in 1982, when wiser heads prevailed and it became a museum and a memorial.

Today the kids will be fascinated by the machines that led to our current fire engines. On the main floor there is a 1906 horse-drawn cart next to a 1944 Mack fire truck. There is even a 1919 "ladder truck" with the original ladders still on it. This truck was used in Ely, Minnesota. You will also find police cars, a hose tower, a brass pole used by firefighters and a unique collection of toy fire engines sure to please the grandchildren.

Upstairs is the police exhibit with a jail cell and the hall of fame, recognizing individual heroism. The motto of the hall represents the people who enter these professions and the individuals who are recognized there: "Heroes are the people who do what has to be done, when it needs to be done, regardless of the consequences."

Many of these people died in the line of duty; others were singled out for a particularly heroic event. Each of them is an inspiration for the rest of us.

Bonding and bridging:

Your grandchildren probably have toy police cars, fire trucks, books about firefighters and many other reminders of these people. A visit here is a chance to talk about heroism. It is also a chance to talk about how society works. In a good community we divide up the jobs and the responsibilities. We take care of those in need and we provide protection against known threats.

What do your grandchildren know about police and fire departments? How about the roles of ambulance personnel, health care providers, teachers and others who give of themselves so that others can be better off? This would also be a good time to talk about how we can help one another no matter what our jobs are, if we will just learn to care.

A word to the wise:

Your local fire department has an array of today's fire trucks and equipment. After you visit this site you might want to go to your local station. The fire-fighters are often happy to see children and will give them a look around. Our grandson, Matthew, was given a plastic firefighter's hat when he visited his neighborhood station.

Age of grandchild: 3 and up

Best season: Mid-May through August

Contact: Superior Public Museums, 906 East Second Street, Superior, WI 54880 • (715) 394-5712
www.superiorpublicmuseums.org/firehouse

Also check out:

The Building for Kids, Appleton: www.kidmuseum.org

Richard I. Bong World War II Heritage Center

No one can predict who will be heroes. They do not come from places called Metropolis or Gotham, like Superman and Batman; they come from the next street, the town down the road. They are firemen, policemen, your neighbors and the military. Heroes are created by circumstances that highlight their strength, resolve and dedication. World War II made heroes of many people who were just neighbors back home. One of these was Richard Bong, born in Superior, Wisconsin, who became a Flying Ace and downed a record forty enemy airplanes with his P-38 fighter plane.

Located along Highway 2 on Superior's shoreline, the Richard I. Bong World War II Heritage Center is impressive but unassuming. It is a modest memorial to greatness and a place where grandparents and grandchildren can explore the horrors of war, the dedication of a nation to a great cause and the sacrifices of both the nation and its individuals in combating evil. That is what comic books are about, but here it is real, a place where you can help the children explore strong concepts through the films and exhibits.

This is a small museum and takes very little time to walk through, but it takes a lot of time to think about what you see. Look at the posters and the planes with your grandchildren. Ask them questions. Have conversations.

A simple "farm boy," Richard Bong came home to marry his sweetheart Marge (check out the name on the P-38) and settled back into his Wisconsin life, but he was soon whisked to Washington, D.C., to receive the nation's highest recognition: the Medal of Honor. Six months later he died as a test pilot.

You can learn about Bong's life, but the memorial is to all World War II vets, and the story of the war in the Pacific is still not well known. The exhibit is a good place to begin to understand. For your grandchildren this is a leap in time and location, so you will need to help them take it in.

If your grandchildren are inspired by this exhibit, explore the collection of oral histories. Let them hear the words and, if possible, come back for the annual Bong World War II Heritage Festival (contact the center for details) where they will hear from vets, see reenactments and watch fly-overs.

Bonding and bridging:

Whether you were in World War II or had parents involved, to our grandchildren this is ancient history and we are the bridge. My father served in New Guinea, but he left his stories and his experiences there. To learn about what these men went through, we need the help of an exhibit like this.

For our grandchildren war is a complex subject. War has no logic. It takes a terrible toll on all people—both in and out of the military. Those who fought should be honored, but we should also help children understand that their goal of ending war was an honorable idea then and a goal we should strive for now.

A word to the wise:

Our lives are collections of stories, and personal stories often have the most impact. After visiting the memorial, share the stories of war and military service in your family. It is also good to share the story of war protesters and anti-war efforts in the family. Both groups should be honored because both were trying to do something right, and it is just as patriotic to serve as it is to try to correct what you perceive to be wrong. That is the real value we strive for in America.

Age of grandchild: All

Best season: All

Contact: Richard I. Bong World War II Heritage Center,
305 Harbor View Parkway, Superior, WI 54880
(888) 816-9944 • www.bongheritagecenter.org

Also check out:

The High Ground, Neillsville: (715) 743-4224 • www.thehighground.org

Superior's Harbor

Who could believe that a state in the middle of the continent would have two sides as coastlines? Wisconsin is lucky to have just that, on two of the top four freshwater lakes in the world. These are Great Lakes in many ways and each coastline is a repository of stories and images, different in context and history. To explore them is to step into the flow of both nature and human history and Superior, Wisconsin, is a great place to start to explore the south shore of Lake Superior—the largest freshwater lake in the world.

The city of Superior is filled with names like Allouez and Menard, early missionaries to the area. While non-Indian settlement on the western end of the lake came later, it is interesting to know that Lake Superior was visited by Etienne Brule (a nearby community is named for him) before the *Mayflower* landed at Plymouth. In 1792, the North West Company (fur traders) erected Fort St. Louis, the first non-Indian development and the reason for the name of the river (St. Louis) that forms the harbor. Throughout the harbor area are reminders of the state's history—including a rich tradition of maritime industry that began after the border was established by the War of 1812.

Visiting the harbor area with your grandchildren connects them with this rich history, the lake, the river, the harbor and shipping. They can see active ship-yards that work on the gargantuan freighters. You can bike or walk on a trail system that explores the lakefront beauty and lets you see sailboats in a marina, as well as the big ships—old and new. This includes the old whaleback ship, *S.S. Meteor*. Exhibits and tours help explain this unique vessel and its story in the shipping industry. The area also includes the recommended World War II memorial that remembers the flying ace Richard Bong.

Should you like to add the Fairlawn Mansion across the road from the Whaleback Museum, you will understand how successful the harbor was in the heyday of Great Lakes shipping, as you stroll through the mansion, which belonged to one of the city's early mayors.

It is an area so rich in possibilities that you can create any combination that fits your family interests, including a swim or time on the playground or miniature golf course.

Bonding and bridging:

What makes a Great Lake? Some think that Lake Superior should be called a sea, that it just does not fit into the normal "lake" definition. You might explore this idea with the children. What is the difference between a lake and an ocean or sea? This can lead to a discussion about how important water is to all of us.

Ask them how we use water. See if they connect ice to water and know the difference between salt and freshwater. With the pictures we have of the Earth from space it seems like we have more water than we will ever need on Earth, but we can't drink the saltwater, so we have a responsibility to take care of this precious resource.

A word to the wise:

The Osaugie Waterfront at Superior combines restaurants, picnic tables, bird watching, tennis courts and a swimming beach, but perhaps one of the most vivid sources of daydreams is the Barkers' Island Marina. This is a 420-slip marina; the sleek lines of the sailboats and the clanging of the tackle as the boats sway make this a port with endless possibilities. Watching the sailboats with their full sails and their quiet passing over the water is a connection to every exploration in our history. Here at Superior, Wisconsin, you can get on a boat and sail to any ocean port in the world! Maybe you should go on a day sail or at least ride the *Vista Queen* and see the land from the water.

Age of grandchild: 10 and up

Best season: Summer

Contact: Superior Public Museums, 906 East Second Street,
Superior, WI 54880 • (715) 394-5712 • www.superiorpublicmuseums.org

Also check out:

Richard I. Bong World War II Heritage Center, Superior: (888) 816-9944 • www.bongheritagecenter.org

Wisconsin's Great Lakes Shipwrecks: www.wisconsinshipwrecks.org

Wisconsin Harbor Towns: www.wisconsinharbortowns.org

Adopt the pace of nature: her secret is patience. RALPH WALDO EMERSON

Apostle Islands

Want to get away to an island vacation? Dream of secluded beaches without buildings? Don't look south; look north to the Apostle Islands. These twenty-two pristine islands are in the world's largest freshwater lake. Each island is distinct and accessible only by boat. This is a paradise of wilderness and an open invitation to everyone who has the spirit of discovery still in their soul.

Bringing your grandchildren to this "seaside" landscape is just the beginning. Bayfield hosts a visitor's center with displays, books and the information you need to make your visit memorable. You can choose the kind of experience that will please everyone.

The easiest visit is to Madeline Island. It is the one island that is commercially developed, and there is a ferry that takes you, your car or your bikes to the island on a regular schedule all day long. It leaves the quaint lakeside village of Bayfield and arrives in the oldest city in Wisconsin—LaPointe. It's hard to believe, but this little village was the place where visitors arrived in canoes—not ferries, cars, planes and trains. The island is the home to Big Bay State Park, so you can combine biking, walking and shopping with one of the great beaches in Wisconsin and a hike along the sandstone cliffs.

If you want a more remote experience, try the other islands, accessible only by boat. There are water taxis if you want to stay and camp, or regularly scheduled excursions if you want to visit the historical fishing camp on Manitou and see the lighthouses on Devil's, Raspberry, Michigan, Sand and Outer islands. There are also trips to see the spectacular caves that have been carved into Devil's shoreline.

You can also choose fishing. Chequamegon Bay is Lake Superior's spawning grounds, and that makes it one of the best areas for anglers on Superior. Sea kayaking has become very popular, and there are rentals and lessons right in Bayfield. This sport requires you and your grandchildren to have physical stamina and coordination, but it is a wonderful way to see this region. If you want to feel the waves, wind and water come together, a sailboat charter is the way to go. There is no better place in the state to experience this sensation.

Bonding and bridging:

What is an island? If your grandchildren can describe an island, you have an opportunity to explore a little more about life. What would it be like to live on an island? How would it change your life? There is a wonderful school on Madeline Island that combines grades, almost like an old one-room schoolhouse. The children go there in elementary grades and then take the ferry to Bayfield for the upper grades. Can your grandchildren imagine riding a ferry instead of a school bus? What happens when there is a storm? If the children can't cross back over the water to come home, what will they do?

Why do we go to school? What is the importance of the island school? The discussions about schools are something close to the children's heart and experience, so you can go in lots of different directions in a conversation like this. I would take the grandchildren to see the school.

A word to the wise:

When Wisconsin was inhabited by only Indians, the rivers and lakes were the highways. Look at a map and see the routes they may have followed. From the Great Lakes you can go to the Atlantic Ocean. From Green Bay you can follow rivers to the Gulf of Mexico. Help the children see how the waters of the region tie the state to the world.

Age of grandchild: 4 and up

Best season: Summer

Contact: Apostle Islands National Lakeshore, 415 Washington Avenue, Bayfield, WI 54814 • (715) 779-3397 • www.nps.gov/apis

Also check out:

Apostle Islands Cruise Service, Bayfield:
(800) 323-7619 • www.apostleisland.com

Big Bay State Park, Madeline Island:
(715) 747-6425 • www.dnr.state.wi.us/org/land/parks/specific/bigbay

Madeline Island Ferry Line, LaPointe:
(715) 747-2051 • www.madferry.com

Whatever you love is beautiful; love comes first, beauty follows. The greater your capacity for love, the more beauty you find in the world. JANE SMILEY

Bayfield Apple Festival

How many ways can you say "apple"? How many ways can you cook, eat and enjoy apples? This is the place to find out. Bayfield Apple Festival is the celebration of the harvest in Bayfield, Wisconsin. Here is where you can try apple pie, apple butter, caramel apples, apple pizza, apple dumplings, apple spice beer, apple turnovers, apple strudel, apple cider, apple brats, apple crepes, apple jam, apple sundaes and apple BBQ pork. And one more thing: you can try plain apples—or rather all the many varieties, colors and textures.

The peninsula is home to wonderful orchards that benefit from Lake Superior's steady cool temperature that holds off frost. If an apple a day kept the doctor away, Bayfield would be a bad place for medical professionals because it is one of the best places to grow these wonderful fruits, and the first weekend of October is the time of year to taste and celebrate.

The festival is a combination parade, party, carnival and feast rolled in to one weekend. With the backdrop of the Apostle Islands and the historic architecture of Bayfield, it is the perfect place to celebrate fall colors and crisp, crunchy flavors. The orchards are here, musicians are here, massive animals roam the streets with feet that are suspiciously human, and a barrage of smells will tempt, tease and cause you to eat too much.

There are over forty-five orchards in the area and numerous artisans who vie for good spaces in one of the ten best fall festivals in the U.S. according to the Society of American Travel Writers. Your grandchildren will be intrigued by the motion, the smells, the tastes, the parade, the music, the rides and the amazing celebration that surrounds one special fruit.

Between trips to the orchards, a kid's carnival, boat cruises, a boat parade and a street parade, events are going in all directions and times, and there is little time to be bored (or rest).

Make sure you pace yourselves. Sit and watch the crowd go by. Let the events and the food settle, and move at a leisurely pace that will let you end the day tired and satisfied rather than exhausted and unhappy.

Bonding and bridging:

What we eat does make a difference, and an apple is a food that is sweet and tasty and also good for us. On the average, Americans eat one apple a day. We know there is vitamin C in apples, but health authorities also tell us that it lowers blood cholesterol, improves bowel function and reduces risk of stroke, prostate cancer, Type II diabetes and asthma.

All of those things are important to grandparents but may not mean a lot to grandchildren. However, it is nice to make a point that the old cliché "we are what we eat" has some truth in it, and we need to think about the kind of food or junk food that we put in the body. With apples, we do not have to eat only things that taste bad or look funny to be healthy. We need to think about what we eat and how we want our bodies to look and function.

A word to the wise:

Many of the orchards offer "pick your own" apples. This wonderful addition to the Apple Festival is one that connects your grandchildren with the source of the apples. When we buy food packaged in multiple layers of plastic or cardboard, children may not know where their food comes from. If they pick apples, they associate the fruit with the tree, the tree with the land and the land with the farmer. It is an important connection and makes eating an apple educational and fun.

Age of grandchild: 3 and up

Best season: The first full weekend in October

Contact: Bayfield Chamber of Commerce,
42 South Broad Street, Bayfield, WI 54814
(800) 447-4094 • www.bayfield.org/visitor/applefestival.asp

Also check out:

Gays Mills Apple Festival, Gays Mills (September):
(608) 735-4341 • www.gaysmills.org/apple.html

Lake Superior Big Top Chautauqua

What is that big blue tent doing at the base of Ashwabay ski hill? Blue and white stripes on the top, orange and colored flags on the peaks of the canvas and solid blue sides draped down to the ground—is this a medieval festival? Miles from town, up a wooded road, suddenly there is a festival. This is just the kind of exciting location for your grandchildren to experience a musical performance unlike any they have seen.

Since 1986 the Big Top Chautauqua has brought music, plays, lectures, professional entertainers, festivity and laughter to visitors and residents of Bayfield and Washburn. It's a form of entertainment straight out of another century, just like the tent. With nine hundred seats that are usually filled, smiles and good feelings abound. You and your grandchildren will feel the energy of the crowd and the performance.

The performance is live, the entertainers are close to the crowd, and the entire production is within view. When the music plays, you can feel all the feet tapping on the earthen floor. The seats rock. People look at each other and nod. Audience members sing along. Laughter passes from one to the other—even if the jokes are not that funny—because people come here wanting to have fun. The interaction between the performers and audience members recognizes that neither can exist without the other.

The annual schedule includes internationally known performers who bring unique blends of music and performance, which blends the folk and ethnic roots of American music. In addition, the Big Top Chautauqua is on Wisconsin public radio with a weekly performance called "Tent Show Radio."

This is not MTV or music videos that children are used to, and that makes it fascinating for them. When the lights go down and the music goes up, they will be swept into the experience.

Bonding and bridging:

"Chautauqua" is reputed to be Iroquois, meaning either two moccasins tied together or jumping fish. Neither of those definitions really pertains to the extraordinary tent show that developed around 1900. We explore what an evening like this means to us only after the experience is over.

Think of the limited forms of entertainment in the first two decades of the 1900s. How does this tent show compare to what we have today? What do children like? What kind of music do they listen to? Where do they look for entertainment? Is it the TV? How would this program go over on TV? What are the differences between live and recorded performances? Could they feel the sounds? What did they like most? Maybe you will be lucky, and you will expand on their definition of entertainment.

A word to the wise:

As great as the music is, the most fun for the family is the historic play called *Riding the Wind*. You will never find a better way to teach your grandchildren about the history of the area. The tunes stay in your mind and reinforce the experience. Live action, projected historical photos and original music make this a really great evening. The programs are so good that the Big Top has a weekly radio program that relies on your imagination to provide the tent and the ambiance.

Age of grandchild: 9 and up

Best season: Summer

Contact: Lake Superior Big Top Chautauqua, 101 West Bayfield Street, Washburn, WI 54891 • (715) 373-5552 • www.bigtop.org

Also check out:

Milwaukee Irish Fest, Milwaukee: www.irishfest.com

Summerfest, Milwaukee: www.summerfest.com

To our children we give two things:
one is roots, the other wings. Andy Rooney

Lumber Camps

There is something special about Highway 8. It not only crosses the state, it connects two of the state's most enjoyable logging camps, and considering the competition, being the best in this category really means something.

Rhinelander and Laona give you and your grandchildren special opportunities to take in the color and mystique, as well as the actual history of logging and the early days of territorial and state history. It was the white pines and the extensive forests that brought men to the cook shanties and camps of Knapp, Stout and Company, and other lumber companies.

Lots of food, lots of hard work, sleeping at least two to a bunk, no room for luggage, and little to entertain—this was a challenging lifestyle that gave the men lots of time to think but little time to have new adventures. So instead, they would share tales of the past, tales of legends like Paul Bunyan and the Blue Ox, and even the tales of the Hodag.

At the Rhinelander Logging Museum, you will see the camp, the saws, the buildings and the tools, but more important you can show your grandchildren the legendary and ferocious Hodag—a beast found only in these woods and only by loggers with a good imagination. The Hodag is "a beast that roars, with the head of a bull, the grinning face of a giant man, thick short legs set off by huge claws, the back of a dinosaur and a long tail with a spear at the end."

After this experience go down the road to Laona and board the Lumberjack Steam Train that will have your grandchildren thinking about "the little engine that could." Climb into one of the two passenger cars or three cabooses and steam through the forest to the lumber camp and camp farm.

Your grandchildren can explore the logging history and enjoy the farm's petting zoo. There is also a nature center, a chance to walk the woods, a restaurant and a blacksmith shop.

From tall tales and tough work to steam engines and forests, there is something everyone can enjoy.

Bonding and bridging:

What are tall tales? Why do people tell them? The story of the Hodag comes from lumberjacks entertaining one another and scaring the city slickers, but it is also the story of trickster Gene Shepard, who played on the people's gullibility and set up a display to see a captured Hodag. In a dark tent with the creature at a distance that would challenge the best eyesight, Gene stretched a hide over a stump with cattle horns all over its body. People paid their ten cents to see the monster and Gene's kids pulled the wires to make the skin move and created roars to shock the on-lookers. They saw what they wanted to see and went away convinced the Hodag was real.

Today advertisers and films still use tall tales and hoaxes to engage us. The films entertain, while ads portray what we want to see, so we will buy the product thinking we will look like the person in the photo. We see what we want to see.

A word to the wise:

A visit to the library might be a good follow-up. There are books on Paul Bunyan and Babe the Blue Ox. You might look for Tony Beaver, a southern logging hero and acquaintance of Paul. There are even a few books on the Hodag. Well-illustrated stories add to children's imagination and creativity. You can also look for references to the bedcats—a cross between bedbugs and wild cats. In addition, you can find references to other heroes of folklore like Johnny Appleseed, Pecos Bill and John Henry.

Age of grandchild: 3 and up

Best season: Summer

Also check out:

Camp 5 and the Lumberjack Steam Train, Laona: (800) 774-3414 • www.camp5museum.org

Paul Bunyan Logging Camp Museum, Eau Claire: www.paulbunyancamp.org

Rhinelander Logging Museum: www.rhinelander-resorts.com/loggingmus/logging.htm

Grandparents are made in Heaven, born with the birth of their first grandchild. GAIL LUMET BUCKLEY

Ice Age National Scenic Trail

As the Ice Age Foundation says on its website, "The Ice Age National Scenic Trail is a thousand-mile footpath—entirely within Wisconsin—that celebrates the legacy of the Ice Age. Diverse geological features along the Trail rank among the finest examples of continental glaciation anywhere in the world. Beyond any textbook, the Ice Age Trail lets us see and touch glacial history."

How much you do depends upon interest, time and the physical condition of you and your grandchildren. Walking with grandchildren is one of the true pleasures of life. We can focus on one another and on the land around us. The Ice Age Trail is a network of hiking options throughout Wisconsin that lets you choose the hike and the terrain that best fits your own needs.

We have many ways to describe a hike. But a really good hike is a combination of exercise, companionship and observation. Our grandchildren are growing up in a era of obesity and poor health, so how do we get them to enjoy hiking and make it part of their life? A good hike has to be long enough to feel like exercise, have a variety of terrain to give it interest, include scenery that changes regularly so that our curiosity is engaged and be a change of pace from our daily lives.

For adults it allows us to clear the cobwebs from our brains, to remove the stresses of our daily lives, and it prepares us for the challenges that we face daily. For grandchildren, it has to be the pleasure of being with grandparents, in the outdoors and making discoveries. Their hikes have to start small and grow as they do.

To make a hike successful, plan it well. Bring food and water—especially water. Eat small amounts regularly. Keep the engine fueled. It is much more difficult to satisfy overwhelming hunger than it is to consume regular treats of healthy, high-energy food in small amounts. It is also much wiser to keep the body hydrated than it is to try and replenish a dehydrated system.

It is also a wonderful experience when you are proud of what you did, a little tired but not exhausted.

Bonding and bridging:

Every science teacher wishes they had the luxury of taking their children out to experience and see what they are studying in the classroom. They know that children learn best when they are doing, that they retain their experiences much longer than their lectures. As grandparents we are teachers, as well as friends and companions. Our wisdom is not just in what we know, but how we help our grandchildren to learn.

Let your grandchildren touch rocks that are 1.6 billion years old in the Baraboo and Blue hills. Feel the sandstone outcrops that form the base for Niagara Falls in Green, Rock, Dane, Columbia, Sauk and Adams counties. Think about the age of the glacial landscape that you are walking on: 25,000 to 2,500,000 years old. Maybe the real lesson is about age: the age of the Earth, the age of their grandparents, their own age. Our life is measured by years, but the value of our life is in what we do with those years.

A word to the wise:

Today, there are only nine National Scenic Trails in the system, and this is one of the newest and most spectacular. What does it say about Americans that we value hiking and trails so much? The Appalachian Trail, North Country Trail, Pacific Crest Trail (including a portion named after Wisconsin native John Muir), Florida National Scenic Trail, North Country Trail, Natchez Trace Trail, Continental Divide Trail and Potomac Heritage Trail. These trails are in the tradition of our great historical explorers like Lewis and Clark and Daniel Boone. Wisconsin is lucky to have both the Ice Age and a portion of the North Country Trail in the state.

Age of grandchild: 5 and up

Best season: Late spring through fall

Contact: Ice Age National Scenic Trail, National Park Service,
700 Rayovac Drive, Suite 100, Madison, WI 53711
(608) 441-5610 • www.nps.gov/iatr

Also check out:

North Country National Scenic Trail: www.northcountrytrail.org

How beautifully the leaves grow old. How full of light and color are their last days. John Burroughs

Wisconsin's State Parks

State parks are some of the greatest heritages of any state—the great concept of public ownership, of public access, of public good is represented in these holdings. They are our most accessible connection to the natural landscape, biological diversity and wildness. Best of all, they belong to all of us.

The park system in Wisconsin began in 1900 with Interstate State Park at the Dells of the St. Croix, one of the cornerstones of the system and still one of the "must-see" parks. It combines the dramatic dark cliffs and narrow gorge of the St. Croix with white pine forests and secluded glens that take us back to the pre-logging days.

It took a long time to get the park system growing. In the first decade Brule River State Forest was created, and in 1910 Peninsula State Park became the second park and it is second on the "must-see" list. This is Door County before tourism; it is a wild shore on Green Bay, trails and rocky highlands, overlooks and a spectacular lighthouse.

In 1911 the third park and the third on this short list of required parks became part of the system—Devil's Lake. Here are high rocky uplands, almost mountainous, on each side of a pristine lake. You can almost sense the glacier that sat between the rocky headlands, while its meltwater formed the lake. In the mountains a lake like this would be called a tarn.

Wyalusing State Park was established in 1918 and is a good fourth park for this sampler. At the junction of the Wisconsin and Mississippi rivers, it brings together the two great river systems of the state. The high bluff has wonderful trails, forests and views, while the river bottoms are a complex floodplain filled with life.

The fifth and final park in this brief sampler would be a more recent (1963) addition to the park system—Big Bay on Madeline Island in Lake Superior. It has one of the most beautiful beaches in the world, a trail along a sandstone lakefront and a mixed forest of hardwoods and conifers.

Where to start? Let your grandchildren choose—from these and the entire list of ninety-five parks, because there are no bad ones.

Bonding and bridging:

We all have a perspective that comes from our life experiences and the conditions when we were born. As grandparents we have seen sprawl, but grandchildren have no idea what that means since the conditions were there when they were born. The importance of parks is to give us a chance to explore both the land and ourselves.

It is worth discussing what they enjoy, what they find beautiful, how secure they feel in nature. And it is important for them to see how you enjoy the parks.

A word to the wise:

The boat ride out to Rock Island and the walk to the lighthouse are unusual and memorable. Rock Island is like no other state park; you travel there by boat and when you are left off, it is only by boat that you can return! Other good boat experiences include taking the car ferry to Madeline Island to see Big Bay or taking the riverboat to explore the cliffs of Interstate State Park.

Age of grandchild: All

Best season: All

Contact: Wisconsin Department of Natural Resources (Find State Park or Forest): www.dnr.state.wi.us/org/land/parks/specific/findapark.html

Also check out:

Big Bay State Park, Madeline Island:
www.dnr.state.wi.us/org/land/parks/specific/bigbay

Devil's Lake State Park, Baraboo:
www.dnr.state.wi.us/org/land/parks/specific/devilslake

Interstate State Park, St. Croix Falls:
www.dnr.state.wi.us/org/land/parks/specific/interstate

Peninsula State Park, Fish Creek:
www.dnr.state.wi.us/org/land/parks/specific/peninsula

Wyalusing State Park, Bagley:
www.dnr.state.wi.us/org/land/parks/specific/wyalusing

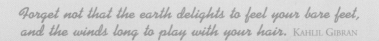

Forget not that the earth delights to feel your bare feet, and the winds long to play with your hair. Kahlil Gibran

Mississippi River

It's the "Father of Waters," the "Muddy Mississippi," the "Great River" and "Old Man River." No matter what you call it, the Mississippi is one of the great assets of the nation. It was the route of explorers, voyageurs, Indians and boats. It is commerce, a flyway for birds, an adventure, a fishing paradise, a maze of backwaters and a watery highway.

Today you can explore some wonderful places on the Great River Road, and in doing so you can help your grandchildren discover geography, biology and history. Take your time; let your grandchildren set the pace.

The Great River Road begins at Prescott and continues 250 miles to a point just south of Keiler. (It also continues into other states, so this could lead to a much longer journey.) Bird watching, biking, boating and scenic overlooks are all part of this exploration.

There are many bird watching hot spots that are also scenic areas. They include Wyalusing State Park, Trempealeau National Wildlife Refuge, Buena Vista Park in Alma for raptor viewing, and Rieck's Park near Alma for the fall swan concentration.

Grandparents who are comfortable with boating can rent a houseboat. If you love fishing, take a small boat into the backwaters where you can combine fishing and birding. LaCrosse and Prescott have commercial boat excursions, and you can rent canoes in Prairie du Chien.

If you prefer biking, the Great River State Trail follows the Mississippi for twenty-four miles from Marshland to Onalaska. On its route you will cross eighteen streams and numerous wetlands.

The small towns along the way are amazingly diverse and fun. Nelson has an ice cream parlor, cheese factory and a sportsman's paradise—the backwater called "Tiffany Bottoms." Pepin is the birthplace of Laura Ingalls Wilder. Stockholm has a great Amish feeling in its shops and main street, while Maiden Rock houses one of the state's largest berry farms and apple orchards.

The best plan is to give yourself time; go as far as you want but not too fast. Explore, enjoy and return often.

Bonding and bridging:

It is easy to sit in the driver's seat with the big front window and the ability to control speed and direction and think everyone is seeing what you see. Well—they aren't. Think about your grandchildren strapped in seats in the middle of the back seat, only seeing what you and your passenger are not blocking. This cannot be inspiring.

You will bond with your grandchildren when you stop, so minimize the ride time. It is the destination that counts. It is the time outside that gives us perspective and sharing. Make sure your grandchildren have the time to really engage with their surroundings. Find stops that are not too far apart and get out and interact with them. Then you will truly share the experience.

A word to the wise:

There is nothing better than an overlook if you want to get a feeling for a landscape, and the Wisconsin section of the Great River Road has them in abundance. Check these out: Freedom Park at Prescott, Buena Vista Park at Alma, Perrot State Park at Trempealeau, Grandad Bluff at La Crosse, Larson Bluff north of Lynxville, Wyalusing State Park at Bagley and Nelson Dewey State Park at Cassville.

Age of grandchild: 5 and up

Best season: Summer through fall

Also check out:

Great River Road Visitor and Learning Center
at Freedom Park, Prescott: www.freedomparkwi.org

Wisconsin's Great River Road: www.wigreatriverroad.org

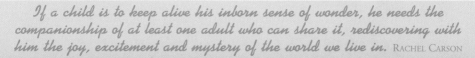

If a child is to keep alive his inborn sense of wonder, he needs the companionship of at least one adult who can share it, rediscovering with him the joy, excitement and mystery of the world we live in. RACHEL CARSON

109

Bald Eagles

Talk about icons! How about mixing the nation's symbol—the Bald Eagle—with the father of waters—the Mississippi River? This is what you can do almost year-round along Wisconsin's beautiful river bluff land but especially in the winter, when eagles leave frozen lakes and streams and move to the open waters and food on the Mississippi.

Eagles do not like to migrate, but they move when their food supply gets low. They kick the kids out of the area when food resources diminish and force them south. As the winter gets harsher the kids keep moving farther, leaving us with an abundance of the magnificent adults, their white tails and heads contrasting with their black bodies and wings.

Cassville joins Nelson Dewey State Park to hold an annual Bald Eagle Days celebration in January, which is a wonderful way to enjoy winter, eagles, the Mississippi, live bird programs, lectures, art and music.

In 1970, when the Bald Eagle was on the endangered species list, there were only eighty-two pairs in the state. Today there are around seven hundred. What a success story! It has been through local efforts to observe and enjoy the eagles' presence that the country took the steps needed for this great revival.

Bald Eagle Days are not the only time to see the birds, but winter is definitely the highlight. Try to view them in the early morning because they are more active and feeding. Seeing them on trees is great, but watching them soar and dive is much more dramatic. You can look for them around the Wisconsin Power and Light site, Riverside Park and Boat Landing, Jack Oak Road and Nelson Dewey State Park. You might also see them eating carrion along any of the roads.

Prairie du Chien has a similar celebration on another winter weekend and provides you with another chance to engage in eagle watching. There you can view eagles between the Blackhawk Avenue and Washington Street bridges, Gordon's Bay boat landing and at the lock and dam.

If you see a group of people, they have probably found a good view. Take your time, make good observations and be sure your grandchildren get as good a view as you do.

Bonding and bridging:

Want to teach your grandchildren a skill? Try bird watching. Using binoculars and spotting scopes requires an optical skill that makes bird watching more exciting, pleasant and successful. However, just putting the glasses to your eyes does not make it work. Practice with your grandchildren. Have them read signs and look at still objects first (you might want to do this too).

Experience has shown us that many people do not know how to use these aids very well. They look down as the binoculars are raised and then do not find the object in the view. Practice makes this work and will eventually translate to seeing the birds in flight. And doesn't this follow the wisdom of that old cliché "practice makes perfect"?

A word to the wise:

Both Cassville and Prairie du Chien have state parks nearby that are excellent for eagle watching. (Wyalusing is near Prairie du Chien and Nelson Dewey by Cassville.) They usually offer trails to hike or ski depending upon the winter conditions, and they also have programs that you can enjoy. These are beautiful river parks with lots of wild land to explore. Check with the park as well as the community to make sure you get the most out of your visit.

Age of grandchild: 7 and up

Best season: Winter

Also check out:

1000 Islands Environmental Center, Kaukauna: (920) 766-4733 • www.1000islandsenvironmentalcenter.com

Cassville Tourism, Cassville: (608) 725-5855 www.cassville.org/eagledays.html

Prairie du Chien Area Chamber of Commerce, Prairie du Chien: (800) 732-1673 • www.prairieduchien.org/visitor/eagles.htm

Wyalusing State Park, Bagley: (608) 996-2261 www.dnr.wi.gov/org/land/parks/specific/wyalusing

Botanical Gardens

In a landscape that suffers a leafless November, a short-day December, all-white January and February, an icy March and muddy brown melt of April, is it any wonder that we are drawn to botanical gardens? Wisconsin is lucky because there are many wonderful gardens throughout the state.

The Olbrich Botanical Gardens in Madison is famous for its Thai pavilion, a gift from the King of Thailand. These sixteen acres include a wonderful rose garden, as well as the Thai garden.

At the Bolz Conservatory, also in Madison, your grandchildren can escape winter in an inviting tropical world of birds, amphibians, insects and fish. It's a fun challenge for you and your grandchildren to find these animals as they blend with their surroundings.

Boerner Botanical Gardens near Milwaukee provide a more formal experience, where the English country garden is mixed with structures produced in the 1930s by artists, the Works Progress Administration and the Civilian Conservation Corps. But don't think that such a place is too stuffy for grandchildren. They also offer Garden Safaris for kids ages four to twelve.

In Janesville you can visit the Rotary Botanical Gardens, with twenty acres devoted to international peace and friendship. Here you'll find Japanese, French formal, Italian, Scottish, English cottage and thirteen other themed gardens. Your grandchildren will love "Winged Wonders," hundreds of living moths and butterflies are released in their education room. Cocoons hatch and children can encounter this maze of metamorphism up close and personal.

Paine Art Center and Gardens in Oshkosh are modeled after King Henry VIII's Hampton Court Palace near London. The gardens include the "Family Discovery Gallery," interactive exhibits that allow grandchildren to explore both gardens and art. They also have Saturday programs geared to children ages five to twelve.

The Green Bay Botanical Garden includes the Gertrude Nielson Children's Garden with a tree house, slide, maze and giant sundial. Think about exploring the Butterfly Garden, the Einstein Garden, the Frog Bridge, the Dragonfly Bridge and Peter Rabbit's Garden with your grandchildren.

Bonding and bridging:

How natural is the connection between children and gardens! Visiting the garden can be inspiring, and if you go in the spring, perhaps there will be time for you to plant a garden outside your own home with your grandchildren.

Putting seed in the ground and nurturing plants, especially food plants, is a great way to teach kids about biology, agriculture and life. It is an exercise in creativity, responsibility and patience. If you want to begin later in the year, grow some indoor plants; let them put in the seeds and get their hands dirty. Buy an indoor grow light and let them measure the growth. You will have a great shared experience that could lead to a lifetime hobby.

A word to the wise:

While the first kindergarten (German for children's garden) was opened by Friedrich Froebel in Germany in 1849, the concept had its U.S. beginnings in Watertown, Wisconsin. The first teacher was Meyer Shurz—her husband Carl was the Secretary of the Interior. The Wisconsin kindergarten began as a German-speaking class. This school opened in 1856 and spread widely. The whole movement came out of the organization "Kindergarten for the Play and Activity Institute." Not bad to keep that name in mind as you explore your grandchildren's world.

Age of grandchild: All

Best season: Spring through fall

Also check out:

Boerner Botanical Gardens, Hales Corners: www.boernerbotanicalgardens.org

Green Bay Botanical Garden, Green Bay: www.gbbg.org

Olbrich Botanical Gardens, Madison: www.ci.madison.wi.us/olbrich

Paine Art Center and Gardens, Oshkosh: www.thepaine.org

Rotary Botanical Gardens, Janesville: www.rotarygardens.org

Wisconsin Weather

As we write this the region is in the midst of a blizzard and while we celebrate the beauty, the whiteness, the soft textures, contrasts and the feeling of living in a big marshmallow, we hear others moaning, complaining, even angry. But what are they angry about and why do we continue to fight the weather? Sure we have to construct buildings to keep us warm and dry. We have to have structures to help us withstand the major forces of hurricanes and storms, but overall, weather is a gift of variety and new opportunities.

Grandparents can help our grandchildren avoid being glued to the forecast and constantly too warm, too cold, too wet or too windy by helping them to have fun in "bad weather." It's harder in the city when the only interaction

with nature is getting to the car, the bus, the plane, the office or school. Then weather is a nuisance, but should it be? Shouldn't we get the most out of all our experiences?

Think back to your childhood. Did you always want to come in when it rained? Getting dirty is normal and not something to avoid. Do you remember running out in the rain, jumping in puddles, making mud pies? Many of these things don't happen now—not because the kids wouldn't enjoy them but because it is easier to bring the children inside. Small children think an umbrella is fun, and they need to walk with you in the rain. Taking shelter under a big tree canopy is another form of umbrella, and it is amazing to see how much rain the leaves catch. Watch how the rain moves from leaf to leaf.

Did you want to be inside because it was cold or snowy? Snowmen, snow forts and snowballs can be fun. It is simple to put a piece of black felt on a board, let it get cold, then catch snowflakes that you can look at with a magnifying glass. We know our grandsons would like to be out playing, and if that is not possible, they still want a fun day. If you can't be outside, if it is really too bad, have some games and puzzles that you set aside for just these occasions, and avoid the temptation to give the day to television or electronic games.

For most of the year, bad weather is caused by two things: the wrong clothes and the wrong attitude. You can help change that. Give your grandchildren the gift of many more good days in their lives.

Bonding and bridging:

Everyone talks about weather, and unfortunately almost everyone complains about it. But what is weather? Of all the events in our world, this is one thing that your grandchildren can observe and study wherever they are.

Tell your grandchildren about the big storms you've seen. Tell them about John Muir, the great naturalist who would tie himself in the trees to feel the wind. Talk about the cold you've experienced and how that would be a warm day to a polar explorer or an Inuit. How hot is it for people on the equator and in the rain forest? What is the wettest, coldest or windiest place in the world? These are exotic frontiers of weather, and if we explore and explain, each day is a new experience to understand and enjoy.

A word to the wise:

While we don't need to fear weather, it is important for us to have a healthy respect for the impact it has on our lives. It is important to dress for cold, heat, rain and wind. We also need to protect ourselves if caught in a strong wind or a lightning storm. Weather has three ingredients: wind, temperature and moisture. But think of how much variety they can create! If your grandchildren can understand the implications of these elements, they will be able to deal with—and appreciate—whatever weather nature brings their way.

Age of grandchild: 4 and up

Best season: All

Contact: National and Local Weather Forecast: www.weather.com

Also check out:

Old Farmer's Almanac (Wisconsin):
www.almanac.com/weatherhistory/locations/WI.php.

Wisconsin Climate Information: www.uwex.edu/sco/state.html

Wisconsin Weather Stories: http://weatherstories.ssec.wisc.edu/stories

Sunshine is delicious, rain is refreshing, wind braces us up, snow is exhilarating; there's really no such thing as bad weather, only different kinds of good weather. JOHN RUSKIN

Dog Sledding

Living in Wisconsin means enjoying winter, or why live here? Of course winter means snow, and snow is the essence of winter beauty and pleasures. And what could be better than a mix of snow, children and dogs? Dog sledding has a very long history and a very practical one. The first dog sledders didn't do it just for pleasure as we do; they did it because that was their transportation and a necessity.

Originally two breeds of dogs were used for sledding: Alaskan malamutes and Siberian huskies. Mahlemut Eskimos bred large freight-hauling dogs capable of pulling very large loads over rugged country. The Siberian huskies originated in Siberia and were used for herding reindeer, as well as hauling loads.

Dog sledding changed as the Alaska Gold Rush created a huge demand for dogs, and any dog capable of pulling any load was harnessed and used until it dropped. It was the low point for all mushing, but it was an introduction to the idea that many kinds of dogs could be harnessed.

Dog sled racing is a more recent phenomenon. The Apostle Islands Sled Dog Race in February starts in Bayfield. It is possible to watch the start, finish or segments in between, since there are designated stopping points where you can ski or snowshoe to see the action. You should be there for the harnessing and all the energy that goes into holding the dogs back for the official start of the race. There is great excitement in the air as the dogs bark and yip and pull at their traces in anticipation of the takeoff. This is a festival with dinners, speakers and maybe an opportunity to try a short dog sled ride.

It's great to get out and see the dogs and the mushers, but your grandchildren will benefit most by getting on the sled and feeling the energy of the dogs and their power. After seeing the race, they will want to experience these amazing dogs themselves. A search for dog sledding in Wisconsin quickly yields lots of websites on all aspects of the sport, including the ones listed in this section. There are many sites around the state that offer dog sled rides of various lengths. You can arrange outings from a half-hour ride to excursions of two, three or more days.

Bonding and bridging:

Kids, animals and grandparents—that's the big three! Mix in winter scenery, adventure and exercise and you have a wonderful experience.

The lesson in dog sledding is the relationship we have with our animals. Whether we raise them for food, work or pleasure, animals deserve to be treated well. The old day of the whip and abuse should be a bad memory that never returns. Watching the mushers work with their dogs will inspire questions about what we ask animals to do for us. Is it fair? Are the animals happy? If so, how can we tell? Many children have pets of one sort or another and grandparents often do, too. These activities give us a chance to talk about why these animals are important in our lives and whether we are providing them with the right care and attention. How often does the dog get walked? Who cleans the cat's litter box?

A word to the wise:

Talk about your pets at home. The grandchildren may be ready to tie something to the dog and expect that the pet will become a demon-puller. This is dangerous for the dog, and you need to share with your grandchildren the danger of putting something around the dog's neck. See how the harnesses work; there is no pressure on the throat. When people tie something around the animal's neck and put pressure on it, it is equivalent to strangling. The dog's windpipe can be crushed.

Age of grandchild: All

Best season: Winter

Contact: Apostle Islands Sled Dog Race (Bayfield Chamber of Commerce),
42 South Broad Street, Bayfield, WI 54814
(715) 779-3335 • www.bayfield.org/visitor/dogsled.asp

Also check out:

Dog Sled Rides in Wisconsin: www.dogsledrides.com/wisconsin.php

Wolfsong Adventures in Mushing, Bayfield:
(715) 779-5561 • www.wolfsongadventures.com

It's funny what happens when you become a grandparent. You start to act all goofy and do things you never thought you'd do. It's terrific. Mike Krzyzewski

Winter Festivals

Northerners have always taken extra pride in their ability to live in the extremes. We flaunt our wind chill like a badge of honor. What? Twenty below is cold? Let me tell you about wind chill. Do you know what that means? It means that if you stood naked and let the wind blow over your body you would freeze faster than if the wind did not blow. And do we stand naked? Well, you have heard of a sauna, haven't you?

To make sure our grandchildren take the same pride in their winter hardiness, we have to go outside and celebrate the season of snow, cold and ice. We need to engage in the frolics of winter—King Boreas is still alive in the frozen tundra!

Other regions may worry about earthquakes, hurricanes, tornadoes and tsunamis; we worry that the next blizzard might miss us. They suffer from their extremes; we play in them. Communities like Manitowish Waters, Minocqua, Park Falls and Wausau gather together to frolic in the snow, to ice fish (the true northerner does not need a fish house), snowshoe, cross-country ski and snowmobile. We see the whiteness of the snow as purity, not cold. We celebrate the clear blue sky, the snow-draped conifers and the tracks in the forest.

This is our element, and we celebrate it with the winter carnival or the winter festival. We carve palaces in ice, make s'mores over a winter campfire, bowl with frozen turkeys, ride in horse-drawn sleighs and crown ice royalty. The winter festival is a creative exercise for the planners, and the only thing to do with your grandchildren is bundle up, laugh and join in.

They will enjoy all the craziness, but here the dogs are a special treat. These companions participate in sled dog races, rides and skijoring. Their spirit is likely to excite ours as we enjoy the inspiration of snowflakes and ice-covered lakes. We may be bundled up and look like weebles, but we are filled with laughter and rosy-cheeked. This is the north country experience.

Bonding and bridging:

It is easy for grandchildren to spend the winter inside watching TV, playing video games, curled up and waiting for spring. As grandparents we have grown up knowing that winter was half our year; to enjoy life means to enjoy the opportunities that the seasons give us. Historically we wanted to escape the confines of our home. Now we have home entertainment. Children can forget to even look outside, and if winter is just going from warm house to warm car, we will never see the possibilities that winter presents.

Yes, it is an effort to bundle up, but it's worth it. Set the example. Enjoy the beauty and pleasure of winter. Become the inspiration. The first snowman, the discovery that we make tracks, the winter birds at the feeders are all delights. The festival is an easy way to discover these joys because someone else goes to the work of making it all happen.

A word to the wise:

Start with a snowman and then visit a winter festival where the art of snow sculpture is taken to grandiose heights. If you time it right, you may even get a chance to see the artists in progress as they carve through the blocks of hard-packed snow and their creations take shape. Some are built as large as houses or castles, while others are human (or gnome) sized. Dragons, mushrooms, mythical characters, Viking ships—the variety is as diverse and eclectic as those who shape them. It's a tricky and weather-dependent event, but it will provide both you and your grandchildren lots of fun and possibly some ideas for snow art of your own.

Age of grandchild: All

Best season: Winter

Also check out:

American Birkebeiner, Cable: www.birkie.com

Klondike Days, Eagle River: www.klondikedays.org

Minocqua Area Chamber of Commerce, Minocqua: www.minocqua.org

County Fair

If you want to have a wonderful time watching people have fun, county fairs cost less, are less intense and are more expressive of Americana than other entertainment events. At the county fair we see neighbors gather, talk, laugh and enjoy themselves. It is a place for your neighbor's child to win a ribbon, your friends to show their sheep. The entertainment is low key—a midway of second-class rides and carnies trying to sucker you into their booths to win a teddy bear. This is the way it was in the 1950s, and hopefully it will still be like this in 2050.

Start the trip by bringing your grandchildren to the petting zoo. Kids love animals, and the chance to pet bunnies, lambs, calves and puppies is irresistible. Next, go to the 4-H building and the livestock barns. Show your grandchildren the blue-ribbon animals and take some photos. (Remember to have your grandchildren wash their hands when they are finished.)

Visit the midway for some thrills. Spin, roll, slide and do whatever your stomach can stand, then let the child go and you be the cheerleader. The Ferris wheel is an old-fashioned ride that still is a winner, as is a merry-go-round. Don't forget the tractors and the booth promoting your local candidates. Eat and eat and eat at local food stalls and the "rolling-on-the-road-every-week" stands. This is not going to be high cuisine, or even healthy food, so take a breath and let your grandchildren taste their favorites. Mini donuts mix with burritos, french fries with lemonade, milk stands and hotdogs.

The bingo caller echoes from one tent and the Percheron horses make everyone feel short. There are contests for animals in the ring and car races in the grandstand. Tractors pull trailers for local transit.

There are implements, canned goods, blacksmiths and floral arrangements on display. You can dunk a neighbor, win a ribbon, eat cotton candy and line up for a satellite toilet. Bands play, the crowd buzzes, the grandstand cheers and loudspeakers blare.

Everyone is surprised to see everyone even though they see the same everyone every day. Is this innocence? Is this the simple life? It is a pace that the state fair can only hope to replicate in little doses.

Bonding and bridging:

County Fairs are really at your grandchildren's level. The crowds, costs and sophistication are less—the demand for bigger, faster, newer not much of a factor. At the county fair there is time to do most everything, and that means pacing. Perhaps the best part of the event for grandparents to share is the livestock judging and the animal performance. This is a place where pride is evident in the owners, in judging and participating. Ask your grandchildren whether they think the animals enjoy this. What is the bond between the people and their livestock? Are they the same as pets?

With older kids you can explore what it must be like to raise, train and groom an animal that you know is scheduled to be killed for the table. This is a complex issue, one that they will eventually have to wrestle with as they grow older. It's good to talk about it in a casual way.

A word to the wise:

There are many activities in which the entrants are kids just like your grandchildren. These might be 4-H or scouts, but whatever the reason for entering, it is something that your grandchildren can relate to. Let them look at the work of other kids, and then ask them if they would ever like to enter something in the fair.

Age of grandchild: All

Best season: Summer through early fall

Also check out:

Wisconsin 4-H Youth Development: www.uwex.edu/ces/4h

Wisconsin County Fairs: www.wisconline.com/attractions/fairs.html

Wisconsin State Fair, West Allis: www.wistatefair.com

Grandparents and grandchildren are God's gift to each other. UNKNOWN

Cooking Together

Food comes from the grocery store! A little too simple, but a common belief among a large portion of our urban children who do not see farms regularly, who do not hunt, fish or even cook! Grandparents have the opportunity to turn the kitchen into a science center. All cooking requires reading—recipes; it involves math—measuring; and science—the interaction of compounds. So jump in, set aside the time, and take your grandchildren on a new path.

Cooking with your grandchildren will add memories of all sorts, but try to make them positive memories. Depending upon their age you can let them use a cookie cutter, decorate your creations or engage them in measuring, mixing, baking and of course eating!

As you search for appropriate recipes, be prepared to do most of the work. If they get bored and wander off, don't force them back. They will come back for the tasting. Be patient and let them get intrigued. Success comes from following some simple rules.

Choose a recipe that your grandchildren will like. This should be a very simple recipe to start, but in one case, we chose complex and challenging recipes to teach a teenager who really wanted to learn. She was motivated by the challenge.

Put an apron on everyone (we know that aprons are getting harder to find) and wash hands. Good hygiene is important and might be tough to achieve, but keep it in mind.

Set out the ingredients. The last thing you want to do is make them wait while you sort out your cupboards. Set up stations that keep the children away from sharp knives and hot pans. There will be three stations: one for mixing ingredients, the oven or stove for cooking and another for decorating or serving the results. Have a stool if necessary, so they are even with the counter and not stretching. Help them measure, but do it over a separate bowl so that extra ingredients do not fall into your final product.

For younger children, decorating is the most fun, although eating ranks high. In fact, dough may start disappearing before it gets to the oven. How can you beat an activity that is tactile, has great smells, looks good and tastes great, too?

Bonding and bridging:

"Build kids not cookies." This is all about sharing and creating. They are learning where food comes from, they are doing something that has a great outcome, and they are beginners. Do not even think of doing this unless you are going to invest the time. Do not rush, do not make phone calls or do other distracting activities. This is not a time for multi-tasking but a time for concentration.

When the final products are done, especially baked goods, there is the lesson of delayed gratification while you wait for your creation to cool before you eat it. Think of some things you can do during this time, like cleaning up the area and dishes you used. Share the patience we need with food—the ripening of fruit, the preparation for barbequing.

You might work on setting a nice place at the table and creating a fun drink while you wait.

A word to the wise:

A good beginning exercise for young kids is making play dough. All you need is seven to eight cups of flour, three cups of salt, three tablespoons of cream of tartar, a fourth cup of vegetable oil, four cups of hot water and some food coloring. Mix the flour, oil and cream of tartar, then add oil and water and knead. Break up the dough into small units so you can make different colors when you knead. You might do this while cookies are baking; it is a wonderful way to create and occupy impatient bakers.

Age of grandchild: 3 and up

Best season: All

Also check out:

The Cooking Store, Brookfield: www.thecookingstore.us

Home and Family Network:
www.homeandfamilynetwork.com/food/kids.html

Prepared Pantry: www.preparedpantry.com/bakingwithkidsinfopage.htm

Robin Hood Flour: www.robinhood.ca/bwk.kidfriendly.asp

Each day of our lives we make deposits in the memory banks of our children. CHARLES R. SWINDOLL

Pow Wow

No one knows how pow wows began, although there are many theories. The word "pow wow" is believed to be from the Narrganzeet Tribe, referring to a curing ceremony. Some think that pow wows were started by the war dance society of the Ponca. The First Nation in Canada website says, "Songs and dances that signified spirituality and religion were used in ceremonies. Upon seeing these ceremonies, the early European explorers thought 'pow wow' was the whole dance when it actually referred to healers and spiritual leaders by the Algonkian phrase *Pau Wau*."

At a pow wow, I see happiness displayed in dance and music, conversation and action. Native costumes are worn as an expression of continuity and promise. There is no replacing the experience. For your grandchildren and you, attending a pow wow is just like being transported to another world.

Pow wows consist of social dances that have special meanings for the nations and their histories. From the very beginning, your grandchildren will be captivated. As the Grand Entry opens the pow wow, the eagle staff leads a flag procession (of the tribal nation, the United States, prisoners of war and the military) carried with great reverence. The flags are followed by the dancers—first the men then the women.

The intensity of a pow wow is unmatched. Your grandchildren will feel the drum beat and may even get a sense of traveling back in time, as the music combines history, religion and social norms. The singers are important members of the American Indian society; the drums are sacred and passed on to each generation. Old songs are mixed with new songs, elders sit beside youth at the drums, and the dance includes participants of all ages and genders. Some feel that the drum is the heartbeat, an answer to the vibrations of the Creator's first thoughts as the world was created.

Every part of the pow wow follows a sacred circle that is inclusive and represents the circle of life. Veterans, elders, princesses and organizers are honored, and everyone is made to feel welcome. The rules are simple—no profanity, no drugs or alcohol, no cutting across the dance circle, and ask permission before taking photos. A pow wow is one experience that your grandchildren and you will never forget.

Bonding and bridging:

The United States is known as the "melting pot" for good reason. Our country is made of diverse people from varying cultures and with different backgrounds. A pow wow is an excellent chance to expose your grandchildren to the traditions of the Native people of America. Here you can watch these proud people celebrate their cultural identity.

Ask your grandchildren how they would define their own identity. (This is a tough concept, so help them with a few examples, but don't give the answers you want to hear.) Ask what traditions they celebrate. What are the special days and events that mark their year? It is also a time to remind them that, like the people at the pow wow, we should celebrate all those who came before us and all life around us.

A word to the wise:

Here are some pow wows to put on your calendar: (1.) The Ojibwe Wild Rice Pow Wow is held on the last weekend in August at the Hole in the Wall Casino and Hotel in Danbury. (2.) The Indian Summer Festival at Henry Maier Festival Park in Milwaukee is the weekend after Labor Day. (3.) The Lac Courte Orielles Ojibwe Nation hosts the Honor the Earth Pow Wow in Hayward on the third weekend in July. (4.) The Ho-Chunk Nation hosts pow wows in Black River Falls every Memorial Day and Labor Day weekend.

Age of grandchild: All

Best season: Summer through fall

Also check out:

Ho-Chunk Nation, Black River Falls: www.ho-chunknation.com

Honor the Earth Pow Wow, Hayward: www.haywardareachamber.com/events_honortheearth.html

Indian Summer Festival, Milwaukee: www.indiansummer.org

Native American Culture—Pow Wows: www.ewebtribe.com/NACulture/powwows.htm

Wisconsin Pow Wows: www.drumhop.com/wipowwow.html

Children are like windows that open onto the future as well as the past, the external world as well as our own private landscapes. JANE SWIGART

Ethnic Celebrations

European immigrants, African descendants, Asians, Central Americans, you name it—all of these people and all of these cultures have been thrown together into what is often called a "melting pot." While we are in the same country, living next to one another and creating a delicious dish of traditions and beliefs, we are still like bits of carrots, potatoes and onions—unique in flavor and appearance and proud of our places of origin.

Wisconsin has been a gathering place for many cultures; the result is a state filled with celebrations such as Milwaukee's Polish Fest, reputed to be the largest Polish celebration in America, and the famous "Oompa" bands in German Fest are legendary. Milwaukee also celebrates several other ethnic groups during the year, while other communities may have begun with one dominant nationality and that determines their celebrations, like the Slovenian Picnic in Sheboygan, the Wilhelm Tell Festival in New Glarus and the Hmong New Year in Schofield.

Polish Fest is a mixture of pleasures for the children. Traditional music often accompanies dancing and costumes. All children like motion, color and excitement, and this is a safe situation where they can be encouraged to dance and observe others having fun. It is a place to see how people celebrate both their heritage and the wonder of life.

Add to this the tastes of new foods, which may be a little challenging at first since most kids are not food explorers by nature. Try a sweet first—that almost always finds a good reception with children and might be the ticket to get them to try other things. It's usually best if they sample off the grand-parents' plates first.

Take in the crafts, see the unique designs, watch the crafters at the event, and talk about how the things they make differ from what we find in the stores. Listen for accents. Enjoy the parades, and get a schedule of events. Make the day a mix of roaming, sitting, eating and planned activities. The day will pass very quickly, and you will have another unique memory to take home.

Bonding and bridging:

What is your heritage? Are you just "an American" or are you Czech-American, Chinese-American or some other combination? For many of us, historic locations can be traced only by going back in our genealogy and asking where each ancestor came from. This is a good way to get your grandchildren intrigued about their heritage.

Each generation becomes more disconnected with the origin of their families, and often only their last name gives them a hint of other places. Mike is Czech, German, Liechtenstein and Ojibwe, while Kate is Irish and German. Yet we have pride as Americans and in our ancestral past that gives us roots and allows us to care about all people and places. A festival is a good place to celebrate our family stories.

A word to the wise:

Almost every culture has its own unique type of folk dancing; and children, especially the younger ones who have not yet learned to be inhibited in their movements, will relish the chance to dance with you and the other grown-ups. They may not be able to get the steps right, but skipping and hopping are always acceptable. If there is swinging involved, that's even better. Other adults are almost always welcoming to children in the dance because they realize this is the only way the dance traditions will be passed on.

Age of grandchild: 3 and up

Best season: Summer through early fall

Also check out:

Festa Italiana, Milwaukee: www.festaitaliana.com

German Fest, Milwaukee: www.germanfest.com

Milwaukee Irish Fest, Milwaukee: www.irishfest.com

Polish Fest, Milwaukee: www.polishfest.org

Pulaski Polka Days, Pulaski: www.pulaskipolkadays.com

Wilhelm Tell Festival, New Glarus: www.wilhelmtell.org

Children have never been very good at listening to their elders, but they have never failed to imitate them. JAMES BALDWIN

Music Festivals

How do we introduce our children to music? Do we just turn on the radio and hope for the best? Do we wait until they are influenced by peers and watch them move to a taste in music based on pressure rather than choice?

Music is a basic part of our human experience. We would not have ethnic music if music were not inherent in all cultures and all countries. It's a basic sense of rhythm that allows us to walk and run, and that freedom continues as we look for outlets of emotion and use music as expression.

Milwaukee is the site of Summerfest, the largest music festival in the world, according to the *Guinness Book of World Records*, with thirteen stages, eleven days of music and a million visitors. The multiple stages and multiple performers allow you to sample many kinds of music.

Do not limit yourself to Summerfest either. We advocate taking your grandchildren to folk and ethnic music festivals (they are often combined) because of the positive qualities of the experience. The music has interesting instruments, from bagpipes to dulcimers, that children will not encounter in the normal guitar/base/piano mix of most popular music. Watching and listening to these unusual instruments is fascinating.

It is not bad to go to a rock, country or blues festival, or any other type of music event, but the questions you should ask are:

- Is the music, including the language, appropriate?
- Will there be drinking and rowdiness, where the children will be intimidated or uncomfortable?
- Is the event kid-friendly? Will children need to be too quiet and keep too still?

Milwaukee's Maier Festival Park offers more options throughout the year. It might be one of the busiest festival locations in the country. Every year the site has festivals for the following ethnic groups: Polish, Mexican, Italian, Irish, American Indian, German, African and Middle Eastern. They are open to everyone and combine music and dance with food and culture.

Bonding and bridging:

Your grandchildren begin with a lack of musical prejudice; they are simply moved by the beat and excitement of sound in both instrument and voice. Research has shown that a child's ability to hear and sort out the complex aspects of music develops the brain for complex thinking in other areas of learning and development. It has value for contemplation and individual experience, but more, it can also be a strong social bonding tool. We have music playing in our home regularly, and we have seen this exposure to stay with our children who today enjoy many forms of music and dance. It is difficult to introduce people to music as they get older, so start early and share in the pleasure.

A word to the wise:

Watch or participate in dancing. The movement of the dancers, the costumes and the choreography are unique and captivating. From clog dancing to ceili dancing, each form of ethnic and folk music is unique and colorful. Encourage your grandchildren to dance even if they are in the audience watching the performance.

Age of grandchild: All

Best season: Summer

Also check out:

Birch Creek Music Performance Center, Egg Harbor: www.birchcreek.org

Concerts on the Square, Madison: www.wcoconcerts.org/concertsonthesquare.htm

Festa Italiana, Milwaukee: www.festaitaliana.com

German Fest, Milwaukee: www.germanfest.com

Great River Jazz Fest, La Crosse: www.lacrossejazz.com/jazzfest.html

Hodag Country Festival, Rhinelander: www.hodag.com

Milwaukee Irish Fest, Milwaukee: www.irishfest.com

Summerfest, Milwaukee: www.summerfest.com

It is not a slight thing when they who are so fresh from God, love us. CHARLES DICKENS

Fireworks

There is something exciting about fireworks that is hard to find in any other shared adventure with your grandchildren. Maybe it's the fact that you are actually telling them to stay up late, that you are taking them out in the dark, and that you are going to watch a sky display that is not only colorful, loud and unusual, but something that would be illegal if you did it yourself.

While there are many places to view and even buy fireworks in Wisconsin, it is hard to beat the State Fair for a full family experience with a spectacular array of fireworks to bring the day to a fitting conclusion.

Wisconsin has a lot of other options for fireworks, including the Fire Over the Fox Festival in Green Bay and the reflection of fireworks in the Mississippi River at Maiden Rock, both on the Fourth of July. It seems as if every town has a fair, and the Fourth of July just doesn't seem complete without the explosions and colors of a good fireworks display. But if you can only get to one, Madison has Wisconsin's granddaddy of all pyrotechnics at the Rhythm and Booms celebration each summer.

In some ways, this is a perfect opportunity for grandparents to begin to remove some of the fear of the dark instilled in many children. A perfect summer evening, a blanket spread on the grass of the park, or near the lake, a pillow to put under your head, and you are ready. You build the image that you want to stay in your grandchild's memory.

First there is the night sky and if you are lucky enough to be in a place where the stars can shine through, you can begin to find the Big Dipper and the North Star. Here is comfort in the night, a beacon that can help you find home. There is always a lot of waiting and anticipating at these events. Waiting for enough darkness, waiting while the crew does whatever they are supposed to do, is part of the anticipation and excitement.

Give them your wisdom, but also give them free rein for their imagination to soar. Let them "oooh" and "ahhhh" along with you.

Bonding and bridging:

Fireworks have a fascinating place in our American psyche. They are light and sound and a symbol. Talk about the connection between the Fourth of July and our national anthem. What is it that makes the fireworks so much a part of our nation's most important holiday? What is the connection between the lyrics of our national anthem and our annual celebration of fireworks? Here is a chance to talk about symbols, patriotism and celebration. This is a story that will take time to understand, but the fireworks provide a time to explore additional meanings.

A word to the wise:

Remember that young children are not used to being up this late and that they do not know how dangerous fireworks can be. This is a chance to give them some safety tips in a positive environment. As they grow older the fascination with fireworks and gunpowder will change. How you handle this with them when they are young could be important to their future.

Age of grandchild: All

Best season: Summer

Contact: Rhythm & Booms, 6515 Grand Teton Plaza, Suite 140, Madison, WI 53719 • (608) 833-6717 • www.rhythmandbooms.com

Also check out:

Fire Over the Fox Festival, Green Bay: www.fireoverthefox.com

Maiden Rock Fireworks Display, Maiden Rock: www.maidenrock.org

Wisconsin State Fair, West Allis: www.wistatefair.com

Picnicking

"Let's have a picnic." Such a simple phrase, but it had so much meaning when I was growing up. It meant we were going to a park where I could explore, and it probably meant that we would be meeting my grandparents. Often it was at St. Croix Falls—Interstate State Park—because that was the halfway point between our homes.

The picnic always meant packing food and dishes in a basket, bringing the charcoal and a tablecloth. There would be a cooler for cold dishes and some pop. Then my grandmother would come with a hot dish wrapped in a dish

towel, almost like a turban—I still don't know how she did it, but surprisingly, that towel somehow managed to keep the dish and its contents hot for fifty miles!

This was a wonderful setting. We would greet, bring out the food, and sit and eat in fresh air, surrounded by green plants and open space. It was a paradise of opportunity for an inner city boy. After the food was leisurely consumed, it would be time to sit in a folding chair or go for a walk. Grandpa would almost always accompany me on this stroll—"letting the food settle" was the code phrase for it.

Picnicking is one of the simple pleasures that gets overlooked in this world of fast food, fast service and fast pace, but perhaps it is the antidote that is most needed. Spill something? So what? Get food on your clothing? No big deal. Leave the hang-ups from home at home. Relax. Eat with your fingers! Crack open the watermelon and spit the seeds.

Don't bring fast foods in their takeout bags to a picnic. A real picnic involves preparation and anticipation. It's a meal, time to roam, time to talk, maybe a swim, and then a revisit to the leftovers.

A picnic is also a good excuse to visit a deli or specialty food takeout. Instead of going home and eating in front of the television, pick up your favorite food from a deli or an organic food market. Then head to the park, take your time, enjoy the setting, the people and the flavors of food eaten in the fresh air.

Bonding and bridging:

The way to a man's heart is through his stomach, and that's true for grandchildren too. The picnic is all about setting and comfort foods. What is it that we like about certain foods? Beans in a brown crock will always be perfect, but a picnic needs watermelon as the *coup de grace* to make it perfect.

Let the grandchildren help with the planning and the preparation. See what makes it perfect for them and why. Do you cook brats, roast marshmallows, eat cold foods, or put a fire to the Shish Kabobs? Enjoy the food; explore why you enjoy the food and why the same foods would not be as good if eaten at home. Maybe an appreciation of tradition, food, setting and preparation will follow.

A word to the wise:

The word picnic was known as "pique-nique" in France and later, in the 1800s, as "picnic" in England. Originally it was a gathering (potluck) like a family reunion. Later, after the revolution, pique-niques switched to open air parks, as a celebration of freedom. In England, the Picnic Society gathered with food from all the participants. The German version is "picknick." In 1989, the PanEuropean Picnic was a famous gathering and protest to reunify Germany. Through all these versions it remains a way to gather without having to open your house or cook all the food. What an excellent idea.

Age of grandchild: All

Best season: Spring through fall

Also check out:

Bay Beach Wildlife Sanctuary, Green Bay: www.baybeachwildlife.com

Picnicking Tips: www.fabulousfoods.com/holidays/picnic/picnic.html

Wisconsin State Parks:
www.dnr.state.wi.us/org/land/parks/specific/findapark.html.

It is one of nature's ways that we often feel closer to distant generations than to the generations immediately preceding us. IGOR STRAVINSKY

Apple Orchards

Johnny Appleseed is a real character in U.S. history, but his story has become more myth than fact because he represents a jewel of U.S. agriculture. He did not get to Wisconsin, but the apple did—and in a big way. The apple was not native to North America; it was brought here from England, and people think it was John Endicott who brought the first trees. Later Johnny Appleseed (John Chapman) took the seeds of these early pioneer plants into the western wilderness and planted them wherever he trekked.

The apple came to Wisconsin between 1830 and 1850, and now there are apple orchards in forty-six of Wisconsin's seventy-two counties. The counties of Door, Bayfield, Crawford and Milwaukee have the most orchards.

The apple, cherry and other relatives are all members of the rose family. It is hard to believe until you make two comparisons for your grandchildren. Let them see the flowers in the spring. We have plenty of crab apples in our yards so it is not hard to find them and smell them. Not only are these flowers showy but what a scent! No wonder the bees love them. Now smell a rose. Can you find any comparison?

Later when you harvest the apples, compare them again with the red rose hip and its apple-like texture—yes, you can eat them. Not as large, not as sweet, but here is an important relationship in the plant world that you can easily explore with your grandchildren before getting down to business and collecting the real American treasure. Like the human immigrants who are now Americans, this fruit is the all-American fruit.

Of course an apple is not just an apple. There are 10,000 different kinds in the world and 7,000 of them in the U.S. and, of course, not all of them grow in Wisconsin. But there are enough to challenge you and your grandchildren to find the one you like best. This is a bit of a hunter/gatherer experience because you are not just collecting every apple in the orchard. Your task is to find the right kind and the right color, so all your senses are satisfied.

Bonding and bridging:

Apple picking is an autumn event, and a crisp bite of apple on a crisp day is a perfect combination. Your grandchildren will have a wonderful time going from tree to tree. If the children are small, they will love your help reaching the big ones. If you have older children, they will see the challenge of filling the crates with quality apples.

This is when you can talk about the choices we make. If we let others select for us, we get the average product. If we make our own choices, we have a chance for the best.

A word to the wise:

Regular consumption of fruits and vegetables lowers the risk of cardiovascular diseases, certain types of cancer and other chronic diseases. That should be enough to get all of us to the orchard. These benefits come from flavonoids, which reduces many chronic diseases. Apples account for twenty-two percent of U.S. flavonoid intake. Ask your grandchildren if they think there is any truth in the statement, "An apple a day keeps the doctor away."

Age of grandchild: 4 and up

Best season: Fall

Also check out:

All About Apples: www.allaboutapples.com

Wisconsin Apple Growers Association: www.waga.org/orchards.html

You will find something more in woods than in books. Trees and stones will teach you that which you can never learn from masters. St. Bernard

135

State Natural Areas

We are always looking for the hidden gem, the place no one else has found, the diamond in the rough—and if you are outdoor people who like to share nature with your grandchildren, Wisconsin has done the work for you. Lots of people know about the parks, but the seldom-visited natural areas represent the most pristine places in the state and offer a variety of experiences.

You can take your grandchildren snowshoeing among the ancient hemlocks at Plum Lake and feel like you are in a cathedral for the druids. Or you can swim in Pope Lake Natural Area near Waupaca in waters described as the best

swimming spot in the state. Cold, clear water is refreshing and the picnic area near the lake can make a full day of the experience.

Avoca Prairie and Savanna along the Wisconsin River contains the largest natural tallgrass prairie east of the Mississippi River. Think of our pioneer ancestors crossing the prairies with grasses that hid their horses! Natural grasslands are not lawns, they are an exciting landscape of flowers, shrubs and six- to eight-foot-tall grasses. The stream that crosses the preserve has flooded often and has created a maze called a braided stream topography with low, sandy ridges and small linear wetlands. There are more than 200 species of plants, including large numbers of rattlesnake master, Michigan lily, prairie blazing-star and other rare species. Big bluestem, prairie cordgrass and Indian grass will change your grandchild's idea of grass forever.

One of the premier wildlife and floral landscapes in the region, Crex Sand Prairie near Grantsburg, is another "must" refuge with a visitor center and miles of roads to observe wetlands, open-water areas, grasslands and woods. Take a lunch and spend the day. Get out early and late to catch the wildlife. Have a picnic in the Grantsburg city park and enjoy nature in abundance.

How your grandchildren enjoy and appreciate these places is up to you. They are not going to see all the subtleties you do, so allow them to experience the quality of the land and not the list of species.

Bonding and bridging:

A natural landscape is the place for the purest relationship with your grandchildren, but don't be too surprised if they don't immediately see the beauty, diversity or wonder of the site. Wild animals learn through play. We marvel at the young pups, kits or chicks. But the cute exploration is really a set of lessons that will serve them the rest of their life.

Make sure you let your grandchildren play, too. If you are too serious about your bird or flower list, you are on your own trip and your grandchildren are there as companions. If this trip is for them, you must modify your expectations and encourage their explorations. Adjust your trips as your grandchildren get older.

A word to the wise:

Take along coloring books and field guides designed for children. Engage the children with activities they know and enjoy. Find puzzles featuring plants and birds that you might see. All aspects of the experience should be enjoyable. But it takes some foresight and planning.

Age of grandchild: All

Best season: Summer

Also check out:

Avoca Prairie and Savanna, Iowa County:
www.dnr.state.wi.us/org/land/er/sna/sna68.htm

Crex Sand Prairie, Burnett County:
www.dnr.state.wi.us/org/land/er/sna/sna32.htm

The Nature Conservancy (Wisconsin):
www.nature.org/wherewework/northamerica/states/wisconsin

Plum Lake Hemlock Forest, Vilas County:
www.dnr.state.wi.us/org/land/er/sna/sna26.htm

Pope Lake Natural Area, Waupaca County:
www.dnr.state.wi.us/org/land/er/sna/sna194.htm

State Natural Areas Program:
www.dnr.state.wi.us/org/land/er/sna/index.htm

The human spirit needs places where nature has not been rearranged by the hand of man. UNKNOWN

Local Playground

Grandchildren do not know life without a television, a computer, a PlayStation. They have grown up with technology and have been captivated by it, but a different set of influences developed the creative minds that produced this technology, and today we must be careful that we do not substitute the end product for the real genius stimulators.

We hear people say they're concerned their grandchildren will be bored! Is that a reason to panic? Is it really bad? What does boredom do? It stimulates. When we create active areas with few rules, with open-ended play, we provide the tools that a child can use to combat boredom. Videos and televisions may not combat boredom, they may mask it. A child in a trance may not be a child feeling stimulation.

Playgrounds are the result of a mothers' and children's movement from the late 1800s to the 1920s, an outgrowth of child labor, factory lock-ups of women and other workers, and a general loss of individual freedoms. Today we are lucky that most of our cities have great playgrounds.

Local parks provide stimulation by design. The play is open ended; no single way through the playground maze of activities. No start, no finish. There are challenges that may seem obvious to adults, but as adults we have to allow the children to find the solutions that fit them. Probably the most difficult thing for adults in the playground is not to tell the children what to do.

In fact, children may leave the area that others constructed for them and wander among the trees, play with branches, chase butterflies and enjoy the variety of life. We need to avoid pushing them to the swing, or the slide, or whatever we see and understand. Exploration of possibility is the greatest benefit to playing, and playing is something we share with many species.

Play is learning. Play is practicing. Fox kits pounce and chase grasshoppers and other insects. The agility they gain is necessary when they reach adult-hood. Young wolves wrestle; cats chase, pounce, manipulate. The actions we take, the physical coordination, the mental exercise, the reasoning of process, the sense of accomplishment are all adult needs fostered on the playground.

Bonding and bridging:

Children often want adult confirmation that what they are doing is acceptable. It is good to play with them, but often they just want you near.

Adults can also give permission to explore. You can open up the forest, the field, the marsh. Joe Frost, a University of Texas professor who studies children's play, says, "What is lacking on most American playgrounds are the materials, the spaces and the equipment for other forms of play: make-believe, organized games, creative play with things like sand and water, nature areas and gardens, and building materials and people around who know how to involve children in those things."

The virtual world has implied that the natural world is not safe. It invites people into a fantasy world where even death is not real and not permanent, so we need to invite children into the real world. We need them to feel a cobweb, listen to a bird, watch fish swim and frogs hop. And the playground is a good place to explore connections. From the toys to the land that surrounds them, the children need to feel at home.

A word to the wise:

Richard Louv's book *Last Child in the Woods: Saving Our Children from Nature-Deficit Disorder* links the lack of nature in the lives of today's children to trends such as obesity, attention disorders, and depression. He notes that children have twenty-five percent less play time than he did. Our concern for security now reduces the area around the home where children can roam, so they are more likely to stay inside.

Age of grandchild: 2 to 10

Best season: Spring through fall

Also check out:

Alcott Park, 3751 South 97th Street, Milwaukee

Gordon Park, 1321 East Locust Street, Milwaukee

Little Oshkosh Community Playground, Hazel Street and Merritt Avenue, Oshkosh

Wirth Park, 2585 North Pilgrim Road, Brookfield

Grandparents and Grandchildren, together they create a chain of Love linking the past with the future. UNKNOWN

Cemetery Visit

Grandparents have many lessons they can share better than anyone else. For that reason we suggest a visit to a cemetery, even though this is hardly a typical grandparenting experience.

For our grandchildren, our deaths will potentially be the first great loss in their lives. I know this is as hard to read as it is to write, but having lost a son, at age 21, in New Zealand, I also know the weight of death is excruciating. It is not necessary for us to have a "when I die" talk with our grandchildren, but we should let the fact of death be part of our lives and that will make it easier. You may think religion will take care of this, but it won't. Loss is personal, not religious, even though religion may help ease the pain.

Cemeteries have many lessons and it can be good for you to be the one who helps them learn these. We recommend choosing old cemeteries that reflect history and events, especially the beautiful Evergreen Cemetery in Prairie Farm, with its old white pines and hilly landscape, and the Indian burial area near the marina at LaPointe on Madeline Island.

Look at the monuments, but visit the gravestones. Find old stones and look at their dates. In very old cemeteries, you will find years with lots of headstones for children who died of diphtheria, smallpox or other diseases. It may comfort your grandchildren to know that when they take their preventive medicines and shots, it is because we do not want to ever face these tragic epidemics again.

Are any names in the cemetery familiar? Can you find stories—military deaths or other events that affected families and communities?

We tend to think of our cemeteries as lasting forever, but do they? We lost many American Indian burial grounds due to insensitivity about their beliefs, but some such locations can still be found in Mounds Park, Rice Lake or Lake Shore Nature Preserve in Madison. Calvary Cemetery in Milwaukee is the oldest Roman Catholic cemetery and includes a monument to those lost on the *Elgin*, the shipwreck with the second-highest death toll in the Great Lakes.

The best event to help your grandchildren experience the history and relevance of cemeteries is Prairie du Chien's "Visiting Our Ancestors" cemetery tours in October, when interpreters explore historic graveyards and the stories of the people who are buried there.

Bonding and bridging:

If you visit cemeteries where you knew some of the people, you can relate their stories. Even after our deaths, we live on in the photos, the stories, the memories of our loved ones. This is why we should carry the stories of our family.

It was the tradition of most societies without writing, to orally share these stories from generation to generation. Now that we have books and writing, many people don't think about the stories to share through the spoken word, but not many families have books written about their experiences.

If you have created a family tree, this is a good time to share it. As weird as it sounds, a cemetery makes a family tree come alive.

A word to the wise:

Bring a large piece of paper and chalk or charcoal. Place the paper over the old gravestones and put the chalk or charcoal on its side. Then rub it over the paper against the gravestone. The words and images should transfer without doing any damage to the gravestone. This can go home with them, a unique art project and a tool for recalling what they saw.

Age of grandchild: 10 and up

Best season: Spring through fall

Also check out:

Brookfield Pioneer Cemetery, Brookfield:
www.interment.net/data/us/wi/waukesha/brookfield_pioneer/index.htm

East Pepin Cemetery, Albany: www.eastpepincemetery.com

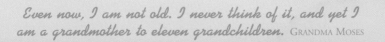

Even now, I am not old. I never think of it, and yet I am a grandmother to eleven grandchildren. Grandma Moses

Nature Centers

As culture becomes more complex, we often lose the sense of place that was part of our ancestors' world. People used to connect with the land out of necessity through farming, logging, hunting and fishing. Throughout the world, elders of indigenous tribes knew everything they needed was in the land around them, that nature provides and they needed to take care of nature so she could provide for them. It was a mutual relationship and it worked.

Then we turned to industry and the cities and people became separated from the source of their food, their oxygen, their water. Naturalists offered people

insight through their writings and encouraged them to find inspiration and renewal by visiting natural areas, but this became a problem as the land became more developed. Around the time of the original Earth Day, the concept of the Nature Center took off. Some are older, but the majority can trace their history to that time and commitment.

Nature Centers, unlike parks, were designed specifically to educate the users about the environment. Created in neighborhoods and in the countryside, they emphasize forests, lakes, rivers or prairies. Most importantly, they remind us that no matter how many stores we have, the basic goods still come from the Earth, and we still need the clean air and water that nature provides.

Find a center near you and take your grandchildren. Connect them with the land around them. Find out how much there is in a few acres. Join naturalist walks, sign up for classes that combine crafts and learning. Sit in on presentations and slide shows. Look at the exhibits and walk the trails. See the place in many seasons. Let them return so they get to know the people, to feel comfortable and to develop a sense of belonging to the land.

Many centers have observation areas; maybe they will be maple syruping or raising bees. Some incorporate farm animals, while others have wildlife blinds. The trails are good for walking in the summer, spring and fall, and often good for cross-country skiing in the winter.

State and national parks are often created to save a spectacular landform and provide for recreation. Nature Centers offer places to learn how spectacular all of nature is, even what we can find in our backyards.

Bonding and bridging:

Many Nature Centers have benches where you can watch birds feed or look out on the forest, lake, or wetlands. These are good places for grand-parent/grandchild sharing. What do they think nature is? Do they think people are part of nature?

What makes a place special? How does this place look to a bird or mammal? What nature is around their home and, can they watch it, enjoy it?

There are no correct answers to these questions. Sometimes we just want our conversations to put questions in the grandchildren's minds.

A word to the wise:

The Nature Center is part of your neighborhood, like a store, office building or home. That implies that nature should be a part of your community. Humans need to learn to live with other life forms just as they adapt to the changes in our local setting. Ask your grandchildren who lived here first. Ask them if they like the birds at the feeders and the things that live at the nature center. Building a good future for our grandchildren means inviting nature in to our community.

Age of grandchild: All

Best season: All

Also check out:

Aldo Leopold Nature Center, Monona: www.naturenet.com/alnc

Brillion Nature Center, Brillion: www.brillionnaturecenter.net

Hartman Creek State Park Nature Center, Waupaca: www.dnr.state.wi.us/org/land/parks/specific/hartman/#nature

Sandhill Outdoor Skills Center, Babcock: www.dnr.state.wi.us/org/land/wildlife/reclands/sandhill/outdoorskillscenter.htm

Wisconsin nature centers: www.wisconline.com/attractions/naturecenters.html

Loon Watching

Is there any bird that can cause us to act loonier than loons? We celebrate them in festivals, gift shops and advertising. Their call is so popular that Hollywood uses their yodel as background in movies, including jungle flicks. But for most of us, the loon is a combination of natural beauty and mystical music and it adds to the pleasures of the northwoods.

There are many ways to enjoy loons. Visit a northern lake and you will probably see one in the distance or with your binoculars, but that will hardly satisfy your grandchildren.

We think that a pontoon boat, which you can rent at many resorts, is the perfect platform. Safe, not too fast, it allows you to come up on a loon and just drift. Cut your engine. Sit in the shade of the awning, sip something cold, listen and observe.

Loons are wonderful entertainers, diving, stretching and calling. They are especially fun to watch with their babies in June, but to chase the loon and make it display is bad for the loon and for future loon watchers. (See "Bonding and bridging.")

Participate in Loon Day in Mercer, Wisconsin—the self-proclaimed Loon Capital of the World! Check on the giant loon statue as you enter town and you know that there is a special aspect to this day. This is Claire de Loon—sixteen feet tall, weighing a ton; she is slightly bigger than the 25-inch, 8– to 11-pound birds you will find on the regions 200 lakes. Claire has been a guardian of Mercer since 1982.

The town celebrates Loon Day in early August each year with a variety of loony activities. With up to 10,000 people attending there is an atmosphere of fun, with events such as loon calling. Give it a try; some people are so good the loons might be taking lessons and others—well, others have a long way to go before they can join the migration. Loon Day has face painting, dancing, sidewalk sales and all the activity of community fairs.

Bonding and bridging:

Watching wildlife helps form a bond between us and nature, and it is something that grandparents can teach their grandchildren. Observing loons or any wonderful animals of the North Country means we must learn how to approach them, how close to come, how to be quiet and how to be still.

People who are good at watching wildlife note how the wildlife watches them and they stop when they see the animals starting to react to their presence. They know that the next step for the animal is to leave and that is the end of us watching the animal.

In some ways, this is appropriate for our lives in other ways. We should watch how the words we say and the actions we do affect other people.

A word to the wise:

Participate in Northland College's LoonWatch, coordinated by the Sigurd Olson Environmental Institute. It's an annual citizen event where "Loon Rangers" report the number of loons they see on lakes in their areas. Maybe you and your grandchildren can do a count on some lakes—whether from shore, on a pontoon boat or canoeing—and participate in the study of this wonderful bird. Some grandparents probably already have cabins on lakes and may not be aware of the program. If so, it is time to start.

Age of grandchild: 3 and up

Best season: Summer

Also check out:

All About Loons: www.northernwisconsin.com/loons.htm

Mercer Chamber of Commerce, Mercer:
(715) 476-2389 • www.mercerwi.com/loons.htm

Sigurd Olson Environmental Institute, Ashland: (715) 682-1223
www.northland.edu/Northland/Soei/Programs/LoonWatch

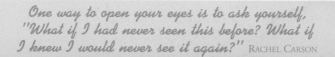

One way to open your eyes is to ask yourself, "What if I had never seen this before? What if I knew I would never see it again?" RACHEL CARSON

Lake Cabin Stay

"I'm going to the cabin this weekend." What a cliché that is in the lake states, but we sometimes take this for granted and we shouldn't. Sure there are many who own lake homes, but what is the percentage of children who actually visit those lake places? What do children do who do not know cabin owners?

Think of all the great memories associated with cabins. Memories of grand-mothers snoring (can you tell Mike wrote this?), of dinners after an exhausting day of playing, sand castles, water skiing, rowing the boat, dipping the fishing line in the water, cooking panfish and playing board games in the evening!

There are many cabins to rent in northern Wisconsin and this is something you should not miss with your grandchildren. It is like "Grandparent Camp"—an intergenerational sharing. A few blueberries from the local woods, a visit to a small town for kids who are the "city slickers," and a campfire on the beach cannot be replaced by anything that plugs into a wall.

At night the sound of cars is replaced by the wail of the loon, the lapping of the waves, the sound of the wind. These are real experiences that will shape the grandchild's view of the world.

Setting is everything. In a cabin, you are in a state of bonding. No need to talk here about slow pace; a cabin is all about slow pace and relaxation. Watch the birds and notice the trees. Talk about the vegetation in the lake that is needed for fishing and preventing erosion.

Good, hearty food is part of the experience and sharing all the kitchen duties actually adds to the fun. This is definitely not a place where you order room service. The combination of individualism, independence, isolation and investigation makes the cabin a wonderful way for grandparents and grand-children to grow together.

But give your grandchildren a little time and space to discover cabin life; they bring with them the influences of their day-to-day life and they need to shed them a little at a time.

Bonding and bridging:

Breakfast is something we grab as we are leaving the house, a pause in the rush to school, work, commitments, yet it is the most important meal of the day and in some ways the most enjoyable. Almost everyone loves a good breakfast. So make breakfast a part of the cabin ritual, especially pancakes.

Pancakes are the classic North Country breakfast food—easy to mix, simple to make well, and fun because you can add anything you want. We advocate cooking together on many occasions, but in this setting, the pride of the grandchildren when they serve the perfect pancake will warm the entire cabin.

A word to the wise:

Boats are part of the cabin experience, but our grandchildren may not realize the skill involved in paddling a canoe or rowing a boat, nor do they comprehend the power and danger of a boat motor. Help them learn. Inevitably you will let them handle the oars, paddles or motor, so take some time to give them skills. Teach them how to be safe and they will learn how to have fun.

Age of grandchild: All

Best season: Early summer through early fall

Also check out:

Travel Wisconsin (Cabins & Cottages):
www.travelwisconsin.com/Cabins_and_Cottages.aspx

Campfire

Maybe it is our most primitive connection, some brain cells that connect us with our ancient cave-dwelling ancestors, but regardless of the source, a campfire is an almost universal place of sharing and comfort.

Camp Fire USA (formerly Camp Fire Girls) speaks volumes about this link as it explains the organization's name—"First meetings of Camp Fire Girls are held in Vermont [1910]. Dr. Gulick chooses the name 'Camp Fire' because

campfires were the origin of the first communities and domestic life. Once people learned to make and control fire, they could develop and nurture a sense of community."

We're not sure if campfires actually created communities, but we have sat, stood and enjoyed campfires in back-country sites, every New Year's Eve and Solstice, and at the Audubon Center where we work. We have had people of many ages and nationalities at these small and large gatherings, and so far, we have never found anyone who does not relate to the crackling fire, the smell of the smoke, and feeling of warmth.

Thoreau said about heating with fire and splitting wood—"they warmed me twice—once while I was splitting them, and again when they were on the fire, so that no fuel could give out more heat."

Making the fire is part of the experience. Teach your grandchildren that a good fire is made of wood that is dry and not bigger than the wrist. Engage them in building and lighting the fire and let them learn to minimize our impact while enjoying this natural pleasure. A good fire is not so large that you have to sit a long way off to avoid the heat; you want it to be the right size to light up your spot on Earth, to welcome everyone in close where they can feed the fire, and big enough to provide heat if needed, or cooking if you want to add s'mores and other campfire food to the evening.

Campfires nurture stories and conversation. Around the fire we lose track of who is speaking; age, sex and other things that work to separate us fall to the wayside. We become equals and listen to one another. Like fireworks in miniature, the sparks dance in the darkness. The flames are mesmerizing and we find our own thoughts—instead of relying on radio, TV or video.

Bonding and bridging:

Humans have a basic fear of the dark, yet our lives are a mix of day and night. Grandparents can use the campfire to help grandchildren fight their night terrors and fears of darkness. The fire seems safe because it provides light and warmth. In some ways the circle of light is like an invisible tent encompassing everyone around.

Have them face out from the fire, give time to let their eyes adjust, and then tell you what they see. Have them lay back and adjust to the sky and the wonderful universe around them. If you are lucky you will hear sounds and you can soothe them with the knowledge that these are not threatening sounds, just the noise made by life in the dark. Finally, you can help them understand that the fire that gives you the comfort for this wonderful evening, is in fact the most dangerous thing around you.

A word to the wise:

If you want to keep building a theme of comfort for the kids, remember how basic eating can be. Something on a stick that allows them to cook and eat is a good way to concentrate their minds on the positives. The old recipe for s'mores—a fire-roasted marshmallow squashed between two graham crackers with a little wedge of chocolate in between—has been a campfire staple for at least eighty years. Megan Janicki is reported to have created and named the concoction near the Ohio River in 1927. S'mores are still a hit today with kids of all ages. For s'mores-making tips and other fun activities, visit the Hershey Chocolate Company website at www.hersheys.com/smores.

Age of grandchild: 3 and up

Best season: Spring through mid-fall

Also check out:

Campfire Cooking: www.eartheasy.com/play_campfire_cooking.htm

Netwoods Virtual Campsite (Creative Campfires): www.netwoods.com/d-campfire.html

Fishing

A translucent line, a hook, sinker, worm and a pole: what a list of ingredients for something that could change a life. Fishing is one of the most basic sports in the world and also one of the most popular. If there is water around, fishing is part of the scene. Of course it is a multi-billion-dollar industry, but fun is not based on what you spend, but rather what you catch, and a sunfish nibbling at the bait is a terrible tease, just as a small bass is an explosion of energy and excitement.

Grandparents need to keep the activity simple. You do not need a massive boat and engine, a fancy electronic depthfinder and a tackle box that needs a block and tackle to lift it. Get the basics and take your grandchildren to the lake or the river. It is excitement and anticipation. Maybe even magic. Drop a worm in, pull a fish out.

Start with panfish. They are simple, they are abundant if you look in the the right places, and grandchildren can experience success in a hurry. If you make them work for "the big one," you are likely to see the excitement replaced with boredom.

Concentrate the first fishing trip on their excitement, not the record lunker. Try for bluegills, which one fishing expert says are, ounce-for-ounce, the toughest fighting fish on the planet. They are enthusiastic feeders, so all you have to do is locate them and they will be waiting in line to get on your hook. Spawning beds are in shallow water near reeds and the best rig is a bobber 15 to 18 inches above a small hook baited with a bit of worm on 4- to 6-pound test line.

You will have to fight the temptation to grab the line and "let me show you." Does it matter if one gets away? Be patient. Isn't that one of fishing's lessons? Enjoy the setting and the excitement and then when you are done catching the fish, enjoy the bounty of your catch and eat them.

Bonding and bridging:

Catch and release is a wonderful idea to teach the children when they are young. This very simple idea shows sportsmanship and conservation, and children need to understand it early. The idea is that catching is the enjoyment, and there is no enjoyment if we harvest too many fish. We need to let the fish grow, reproduce and keep the lake stocked. The idea of filling out—taking the limit—can be an exercise in greed.

Talk about greed, conservation, limited resources and making choices about what we need and what we want. These are important topics. They are hard to cover in normal conversation, but when you're having fun catching the bluegills and have to decide when it's time to start putting them back, you have a perfect setting to explore the idea.

A word to the wise:

If you lack the gear to take your grandchildren fishing, check the Wisconsin DNR's Fishing Equipment Loan Program. This wonderful program allows young anglers to borrow tackle free at select state parks and DNR field offices. Equipment may be borrowed for up to one week. To ensure availability, requests should be made in advance to the specific field office or state park where it will be picked up. Most locations offer reels, rods, casting plugs, bobbers, hooks, line and sinkers. BYOB—Bring Your Own Bait.

Age of grandchild: 3 and up

Best season: Late spring through early fall

Also check out:

Wisconsin Department of Natural Resources:

Fishing Wisconsin: www.dnr.wi.gov/fish

Fishing Equipment for Loan:
www.dnr.wi.gov/fish/kidsparents/loanerequipment.html

Fishing Wisconsin: Angler Education:
www.dnr.wi.gov/fish/kidsparents/anglereducation

Fishing Wisconsin: Learning Opportunities:
www.dnr.wi.gov/fish/kidsparents/learningopportunities.html

One hundred years from now, it will not matter what my bank account was, how big my house was, or what kind of car I drove. But the world may be a little better because I was important in the life of a child. FOREST WITCRAFT

Lighthouse Visit

How many lighthouses are there in Wisconsin? One list says there are fifty! This list includes some privately owned lights on Lake Winnebago and many pier lights that may not be considered lighthouses by some. But then how do we decide what is a lighthouse? Maybe the best choices are those who belong in the old-time photos, the stories of shipwrecks and the wave-tossed seas. They are the lighthouses with keepers who moved in with their families, raised crops and kids and saved lives. Now radio signals coordinate the lights that are still active, but the stories and memories of heroism are still there.

The lighthouses that fit our romantic image and the images in the children's books are usually on rugged coasts or islands. They seem lonely and of course were beacons of hope on storm-tossed coasts. Here the heroic lighthouse keepers worked to keep their oil lamps lit and helped to rescue the survivors of ships that could not handle the tempest of Great Lakes storms. Their setting alone will inspire your grandchildren. They look like a cross between a flashlight and a silo (or maybe a rocket ship).

A visit to a lighthouse begins with a trip to the lake. The journey can include stories or coloring books or maps to help the child get perspective. Take a few books based on lighthouses in the car because, surprisingly, there are still many books on this topic, despite the fact that lighthouse keepers are no longer part of our world.

Many lighthouses on these shores can be reached by foot and the walk is part of the pleasure, since it creates the setting for the lighthouse. Others, like the ones on Rock Island and the Apostles, include the excitement of a boat ride. Inside you may still see the lighthouse keeper's home and information about why the lighthouse was put there and what role it played in Wisconsin and Great Lakes history. The best part is to go up to the light and get a dizzying look at the landscape. Point out to the children that as far as they can see to the horizon, faraway ships could be looking for the light to guide them in.

As you leave, walk around the lighthouse and talk about what it would have been like to live here. Remember that lighthouse keepers often had their families living with them.

Bonding and bridging:

Despite the presence of lighthouses, there have been numerous shipwrecks in Great Lakes history. Today our travel takes many forms and it might be good to share with the grandchildren how we have worked to make all these modes safer. Who are today's lighthouse keepers? Perhaps they are the air traffic controllers, the police directing traffic, the railroad signal men. We have road service, 911 and lots of things we can call on, but everything depends upon our making the best decisions to avoid as many dangerous situations as we can.

As a grandparent you are sharing adventures with the children, but you are also their lighthouse keepers, choosing safety, watching for danger, and willing to step in when needed. Their life is a voyage and you are there to help them past some of the obstacles of growing up.

A word to the wise:

The third week in May is the annual weekend Lighthouse Walk in Sturgeon Bay. If you have ever dreamed of living in a lighthouse, or if you are among the thousands who love the romance of those light beacons, this may be the best event in the state. It starts at the Door County Maritime Museum on Friday evening with the Keepers' Kin reception with great food, presentations and lots of stories. This is followed by two days of self-guided tours at five mainland lighthouses. There really is nothing to compare to this lighthouse extravaganza, especially if you combine it with a walk along the docks and observe the boats in the harbor.

Age of grandchild: 3 and up

Best season: Summer

Contact: Door County Maritime Museum, 120 North Madison Avenue, Sturgeon Bay, WI 54235 • (920) 743-5958 • www.dcmm.org

Also check out:

Apostle Islands Lighthouse Celebration, Bayfield: www.lighthousecelebration.com/ail.htm

An online pictorial inventory of Wisconsin lighthouses: www.cr.nps.gov/maritime/light/wi.htm

Grandparents somehow sprinkle a sense of stardust over grandchildren. ALEX HALEY

Kite Flying

If you are looking for a simple activity that connects wind, energy and flight, it is hard to beat a kite. If you are looking for something that is almost magic—build your own with string, ribbon, newspaper and wood. Can you imagine those ingredients taking you into the atmosphere? How do you shape the kite? Why a tail? Do you run with the wind, against or across? Folks have pondered these questions and experimented with kites since 1000 BC in China, and we still work with the same basic elements to make a sailboat move, support a parasail, or lift a hang glider.

Marco Polo brought kites from China to the western world and the western world used them in practical ways. Alexander Wilson flew thermometers on his kites. Ralph Archbold flew anemometers, and Benjamin Franklin survived a really dumb experiment: flying a kite in a lightning storm. Ships released kites if they were in danger and hoped there would be a rescue as a result, and kites were placed on life rafts to help rescuers spot the drifting boats.

I still have memories of a clear sunny day with gusty winds on a hill when I was a child. There was a wonderful clear field of grass surrounded by a boulevard of oak trees. My parents and grandparents had purchased a box kite, one of the first purchased kites that I'd had. We assembled it and the excitement grew. The breeze blew. I ran and ran and ran and it seemed as if I was destined to have the only earthbound kite in the park, but then it took flight and we were playing out the string, watching it rise, feeling the pull of the wind. We were tethered to flight and it was exhilarating, until finally it was time to reel it in. The kite fought the command to return to the ground and as a last vestige of independence it found an oak tree. My grandfather and my father both thought that they could get it down. Now I wonder—is my dad's shoe still lodged in that oak branch?

There is no better place for kite flying than on the Milwaukee shore of Lake Michigan, which hosts the Cool Fool Kite Festival on New Year's Day with free hot chocolate and snacks while they last. Or you can choose the warmer and maybe breezier Time Warner Cable Family Kite Festival scheduled for Memorial Day weekend and the Frank Mots International Kite Festival on Labor Day weekend.

Bonding and bridging:

What could be more pleasurable and simple than running across a field, string in hand, kite taking flight? This is the joy of shared experience. It is not the money we spend, the glitz and the glamour that connects us with our grandchildren, but rather the quiet sharing of discovery.

What is flight? What is wind? How did human beings learn to control the wind and rise to the sky? Does the kite teach us anything about flight? How perfect an opportunity to talk about Wilbur and Orville Wright, da Vinci, and all the dreamers of flight who have led us to our modern planes and rockets. The kite is our thread to the sky. It was Ben Franklin's means to learn about lightning, maybe it is your means to explore your dreams about the universe.

A word to the wise:

We used to think of kites as a summer recreation, but the extreme skiers have now found out that they can harness themselves to modified kites and be pulled, often airborne, across the lake ice. This is a fun combination of two colorful sports and something you can watch in Madison, Chequamegon Bay, and on other good lakes. Have fun and watch these skiers catch the wind. Some day it might be your grandchild out there.

Age of grandchild: 3 and up

Best season: All

Also check out:

EEA Wings on Strings Kite Festival, Oshkosh (June): (920) 426-4800

Gift of Wings, Milwaukee: (414) 273-5483 • www.giftofwings.com

Cool Fool Kite Festival

Time Warner Cable Family Kite Festival

Frank Mots International Festival

Life is no brief candle to me. It is a sort of splendid torch which I've got hold of for the moment and I want to make it burn as brightly as possible before handing it on to the future generations. George Bernard Shaw

155

Library

A trip to the library is a magical experience for your grandchild. He's already seen and read the books at home. At the bookstore, he's not allowed to touch. But as soon as he walks into the library, he has the world at his fingertips. Few places hold so much potential for so many adventures and discoveries.

In the U.S., one man—Andrew Carnegie—built 2,509 libraries between 1881 and 1917. His philanthropy was mostly in America, the British Isles and Canada. He made this gift to the people because he believed libraries added to the meritocratic nature of America and anyone with the right inclination and desire could educate themselves.

Since then, libraries have grown in many ways. While it might seem that libraries are losing their place in our age of technology, just the opposite is true. According to a report on Wisconsin libraries, public circulation surpassed 56.8 million items in 2004 and user visits increased to almost 32 million. Library use was increasing at a faster rate than population growth!

Give your grandchildren time to explore and find a book (or two) that excites them. Guide them if they need help. Search for books together based on a series they enjoy, an author they like or a subject matter of interest to both of you. Let them absorb the atmosphere. This is a place where book lovers congregate, where a passion for reading can be observed and absorbed.

Do your part and set an example, too. Check out a few books before you leave. Don't spend too much time browsing for yourself. (It's best if you already know what you're looking for.) But if you leave with a handful of books, your grandchildren will notice. They may even ask what you're reading, and from there the conversation can soar.

Libraries offer other opportunities, too. Children's authors make appearances. It's always a thrill for kids to meet the writers who create the characters and worlds they read about. Libraries occasionally host used book sales—a chance to help your library raise funds. And most books cost no more than a dollar!

A library visit holds unlimited potential—so much so, that it may be worth repeating with your grandchildren every week.

Bonding and bridging:

I remember going to the Rice Lake library. It was a wonderful building that no longer exists. This massive building not only dominated a corner on the edge of the downtown, but it gave me a freedom to explore ideas, pictures, even book titles, and it was part of every trip to visit my grandparents.

Books are a repository of knowledge, feelings, personal connections, exchange between reader and writer. They are intimate capsules of knowledge and they need to be appreciated, but how? Maybe it needs to be from a generation who knew about encyclopedia salesmen.

Children who are exposed to books at an early age tend to become strong readers and learners. A fundamental goal of libraries is to instill in people (especially children) a lifelong love of reading and to provide learning opportunities through books and various other media formats. Visiting a library together can foster a special relationship between the generations by bonding over a shared book.

A word to the wise:

A visit to the library can enhance just about any experience in this book. Of course, you can check out *Sadako and the Thousand Paper Cranes* by Eleanor Coerr before visiting the Ice Age Trail. With older grandchildren, you may want to read *Journey Through the Ice Age* before hiking the trail. And let's not forget *The Fighter Aces* by Raymond F. Toliver as a supplement to the Bong WWII Museum in Superior. There are many other possibilities. Read about American Indians before attending a pow wow. Whatever the topic may be, you have a world of books from which to choose.

Age of grandchild: All

Best season: All

Also check out:

The Library History Buff: www.libraryhistorybuff.org

Wisconsin Libraries: www.librarysites.info/states/wi.htm

Grandparents Day

Grandparents are special; we play an important part in raising healthy grand-children and because of that we deserve a day! But our day ranks far below Mother's Day and Father's Day. Maybe that is because we have not stepped forward to get the recognition we need. So we say—step up, make it special and ask that you get to spend quality time with your grandchildren.

Grandparents Day was first established in 1973 in West Virginia through the efforts of Marian McQuade, a mother of 15 who was as dedicated to the care of senior citizens as she was to children. In her efforts to reach out to the grandparent generation of her time, she formed the Forget-Me-Not Ambassadors, to make sure that senior homes were visited regularly.

In 1978, the U.S. Congress and President Jimmy Carter recognized this effort and ushered in a national day of commemoration. President Carter said at the signing of the new legislation: "Whether they are our own or surrogate grandparents who fill some of the gaps in our mobile society, our senior generation also provides our society a link to our national heritage and traditions."

Grandparents Day is the first Sunday after Labor Day, and can be overlooked since it follows the last big holiday of summer, at the beginning of school, autumn and family schedules. But don't let it be forgotten. Instead, make it a day that brings grandchildren into grandparents' lives. Your children can help make it happen, but it can be a success if you do some of the planning, too.

The day is not about going somewhere for entertainment. Have a cake, have a celebration, but concentrate on things that made your childhood special. Play some of the old board games—they are still around, just not as prevalent. Make a rocket ship out of a cardboard box (I bet you can remember doing that), thread spools attached to the box for controls, and crayon scenes for windows. Gather everyone around and tell a story about your childhood and make this a day of photo album reminiscence—but not too much—let them leave wanting to see more, not hoping that you do not find another album.

This day is about you and for you. Make your life and your love the focus for this special time.

Bonding and bridging:

It can be hard for some people to show their true feelings. Saying "I love you" seems almost taboo. Why that is, I do not know. But Grandparents Day is a good time to remember that it's okay to let your family members know you love them.

I was lucky. The night my father died we talked on the phone and I said, "I love you Dad." He was gone three hours later. The week our son Matthew died I told him I loved him. It was our last conversation. Waiting to say "I love you" can leave you empty. So express yourself whenever you can. You will never regret that you reached out to someone special.

A word to the wise:

Choose a special activity like those described in this book and repeat it each year. Traditions are built upon repetition, like Kate's grandmother making chicken and mashed potatoes every Sunday night, or Mike's grandmother making blackberry pie every July. Later we are rewarded by memories that are triggered by an old car, a special taste, the color of a favorite sweater, the smell of aftershave or perfume. On this day of all days, provide your grandchildren with the sensations that will bring back memories decades later.

Age of grandchild: All

Best season: The first Sunday after Labor Day

Also check out:

Candy You Ate as a Kid: www.oldtimecandy.com

Hometown Favorites: www.hometownfavorites.com

National Grandparents Day: www.grandparents-day.com

Sweet Nostalgia: www.sweetnostalgia.com

Grandchildren are the dots that connect the lines from generation to generation. Lois Wyse

Index

About the Authors

Mike Link:

Mike Link is the author of seventeen books and numerous magazine articles. He and and his wife Kate live in the woods near Willow River, Minnesota, with two labrador retrievers and a feeder full of birds.

For more than thirty-five years, Mike has directed the Audubon Center near Sandstone, Minnesota, and he occasionally guides groups through the western parks of the state. He takes pride in teaching and enjoys sharing his knowledge about environmental subjects with the students at Hamline University, Northland College and others.

Traveling is a passion that Mike shares with Kate, one that has taken them to all fifty states and twenty countries. It is the author's belief that if you breathe air, drink water and enjoy life, you owe a debt to the future and must preserve and protect the world's environments.

Mike's son Matthew was a student at the University of Minnesota Duluth when he died in a kayak accident in New Zealand, and his son Jon is a kayak wilderness ranger near Juneau, Alaska. His daughters Julie and Alyssa have provided him with grandsons—Matthew, Aren, Ryan and Annalise—who have given him the gift to see the world again through new eyes.

Kate Crowley:

For twenty-one years, Kate Crowley has lived her dream. Since marrying Mike and moving to the country, she has been surrounded by forests, prairies,

birds, dogs, cats and horses. Her dream was made complete when she became a grandmother.

Kate has been a naturalist, an educator and a writer for twenty-nine years, first at the Minnesota Zoo and now at the Audubon Center of the North Woods. She has co-authored nine books with Mike. She has written for magazines and currently writes a monthly nature column for three newspapers.

Kate enjoys hiking, biking, skiing, scrapbooking, reading and spending as much time as possible with her grandchildren. She considers protecting and preserving the natural world for her grandchildren and for future generations to be her highest priority.

Visit Mike and Kate's website at www.GrandparentsAmericanStyle.com

Notes

Date: Comments:

Date:

Comments:

Date:

Comments:

Date:

Comments:

Date:

Comments:

Date:

Comments:

Date: **Comments:**

Date:

Comments:

Date:

Comments: